A World of Dinosaurs

by **Vicky Woodgate** and **Jon Tennant**

BPP

Contents

A World of Dinosaurs 6
The Age of Dinosaurs 8
Dinosaurs Today 10

North America
Tyrannosaurus 14
Allosaurus 15
Dakotaraptor 16
Troodon 17
Brachiosaurus 18
Diplodocus 19
Parasaurolophus 20
Stegosaurus 21
Zuul 22
Triceratops 23
Pachycephalosaurus 24
Quetzalcoatlus 25
Archelon 26
Tylosaurus 27

South America
Herrerasaurus 30
Giganotosaurus 31
Carnotaurus 32
Eoraptor 33
Patagotitan 34
Amargasaurus 35
Dreadnoughtus 36
Talenkauen 37

Anhanguera 38
Dakosaurus 39

Africa
Spinosaurus 42
Carcharodontosaurus 43
Majungasaurus 44
Massospondylus 45
Paralititan 46
Lesothosaurus 47
Ouranosaurus 48
Kentrosaurus 49
Phosphatodraco 50
Alcione 51
Angolasaurus 52
Sarcosuchus 53

Asia
Sinosauropteryx 56
Therizinosaurus 57
Velociraptor 58
Caihong 59
Halszkaraptor 60
Huabeisaurus 61
Mamenchisaurus 62
Huayangosaurus 63
Protoceratops 64
Psittacosaurus 65
Kryptodrakon 66

Guidraco 67
Azhdarcho 68
Shastasaurus 69

Europe
Baryonyx 72
Liliensternus 73
Compsognathus 74
Balaur 75
Archaeopteryx 76
Iguanodon 77
Scelidosaurus 78
Hatzegopteryx 79
Ornithocheirus 80
Liopleurodon 81
Plesiosaurus 82
Metriorhynchus 83

Oceania & Antarctica
Australovenator 86
Savannasaurus 87
Leaellynasaura 88
Minmi 89
Kronosaurus 90
Vegasaurus 91

Glossary 92
Index 94

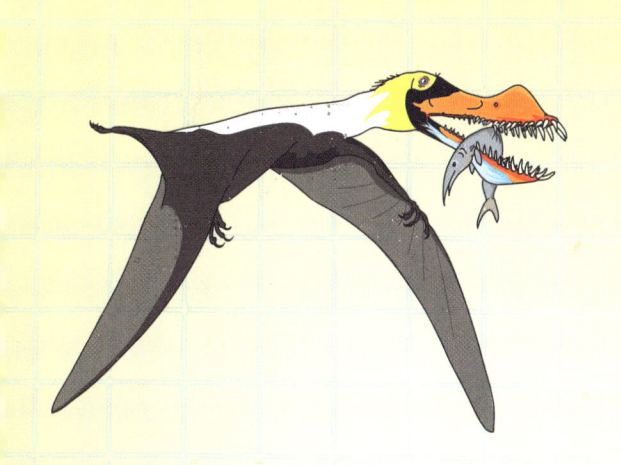

Introduction

Welcome to the world of dinosaurs! This book will take you back in time to an age when reptiles ruled the Earth. Spanning every continent, our journey takes in more than 60 dinosaurs and their relatives – from little to large, including some you may never have heard of!

A World of Dinosaurs reveals the incredible variety of prehistoric life, and shows how dinosaurs once dominated every corner of the Earth. Are you ready to begin your global dinosaur hunt? Then let's get to it . . .

A World of Dinosaurs

Around 230 million years ago, dinosaurs were the dominant life form on our planet. Some were gentle plant eaters, while others were ferocious predators. They ranged from tiny predators hardly bigger than a chicken to huge grazing animals more than 35 metres long. This makes the biggest dinosaurs the largest animals ever to have walked the Earth.

What did dinosaurs look like?

Dinosaurs were a group of reptiles that lived on land, between 245 and 60 million years ago. They all had tails and laid eggs, and walked about on two legs or four. It is thought most dinosaurs had scaly skin, like lizards today.

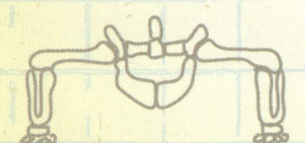

Long tail for balance

Feet and legs positioned directly beneath hips

Scaly skin

Rugops primus
- Name means 'wrinkle face'
- Found in Africa

Scientists can tell the difference between dinosaurs and other reptiles by the complete hole through their hip socket.

Modern reptiles hold their legs to the side of their bodies.

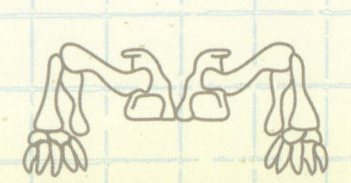

Crocodiles walk with their knees bent outwards.

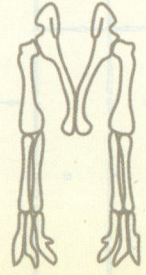

Dinosaurs walked with their legs straight under them.

> **What is a dinosaur?**
>
> Dinosaurs all walked on the ground. The flying and swimming reptiles that lived alongside them were not dinosaurs at all but distinct groups of their own.

Bird-hipped or lizard-hipped?

Dinosaurs are grouped according to the shape of their hips. Ornithischian or 'bird-hipped' dinosaurs had backward-slanting hips (pubic bones), while the saurischian or 'lizard-hipped' dinosaurs had forward-slanting hips. The saurischians were made up of two further groups: sauropods and theropods.

Surprise surprise
Despite their name, bird-hipped dinosaurs have no relation to modern-day birds. In fact, modern birds are descended from lizard-hipped dinosaurs!

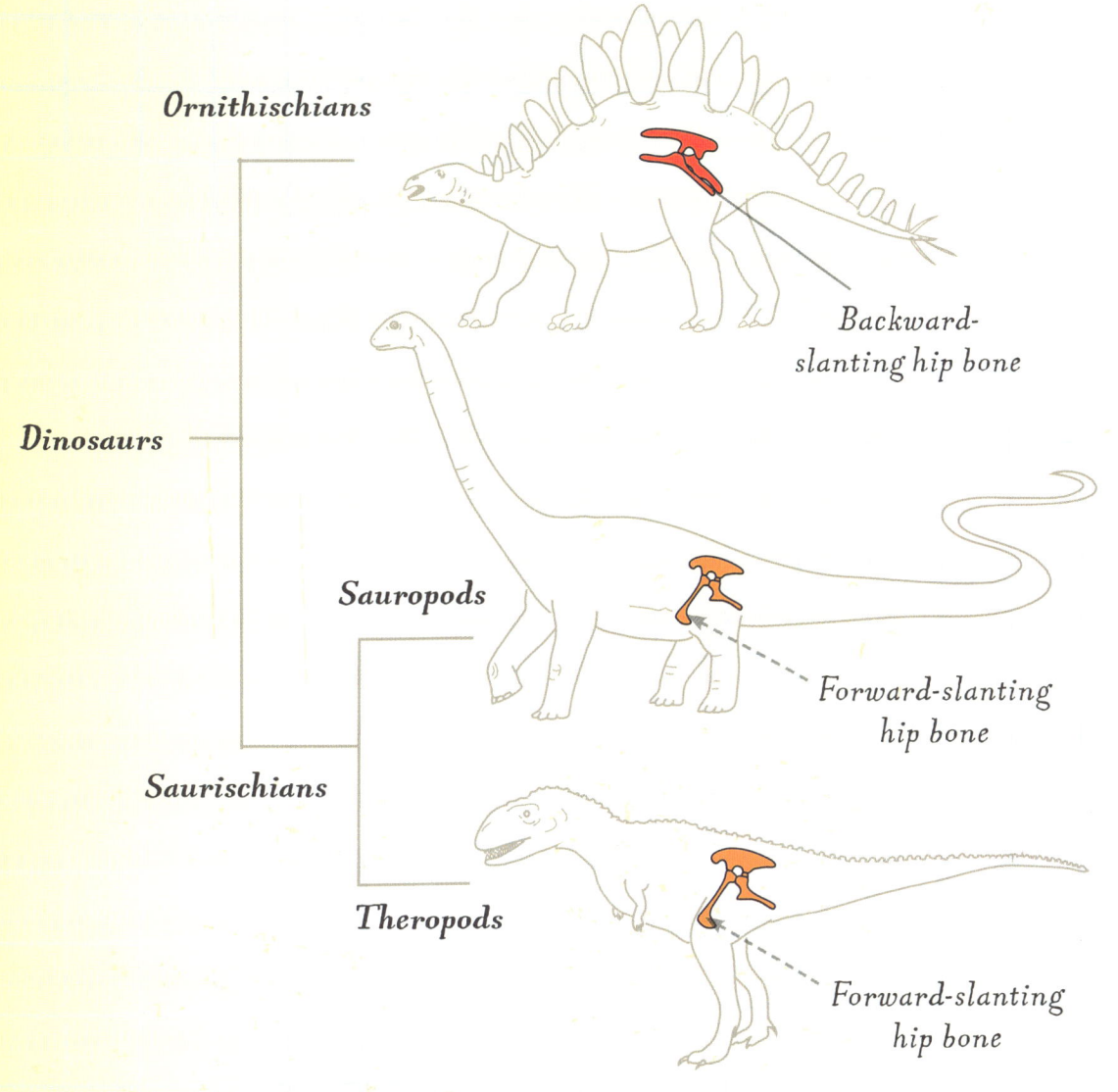

Ornithischians

Dinosaurs

Sauropods

Saurischians

Theropods

Backward-slanting hip bone

Forward-slanting hip bone

Forward-slanting hip bone

Ornithischians
Ornithischians were all plant-eaters. Some had armour or horns.

Sauropods
These plant-eaters were known for their long neck, whiplash tails and huge size.

Theropods
These two-legged meat-eaters later evolved to have feathers.

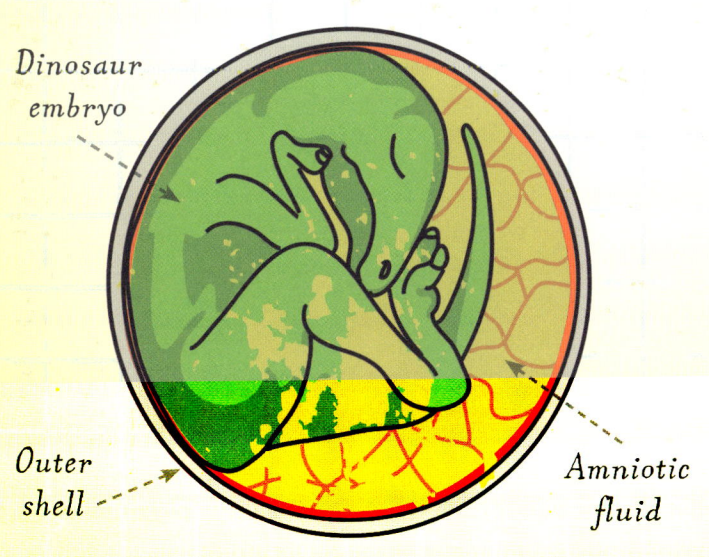

Dinosaur embryo

Outer shell

Amniotic fluid

Eggs
Dinosaurs, like modern birds, laid eggs. Their fossilised remains have been found all over the world. Many of these have been found clustered together. Some dinosaurs have even been fossilised sitting over or 'brooding' their eggs.

The Age of Dinosaurs

The first dinosaurs appeared around 230 million years ago. They lived over three major periods in the history of Earth: the Triassic, Jurassic and Cretaceous periods. Together, these form the Mesozoic era, often referred to as the Age of Dinosaurs.

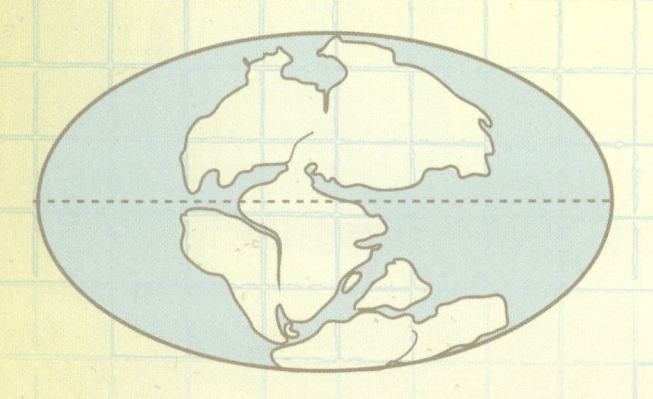

The Triassic

At the beginning of the Triassic, there was one huge 'supercontinent' called Pangaea. Gradual movements within the Earth forced this to split into two continents: Laurasia and Gondwana.

TRIASSIC: 251-199 million years ago

The Jurassic

The continents continued to move away from each other, temperatures dropped and plant life became more lush and abundant. Dinosaurs grew bigger and began to diversify.

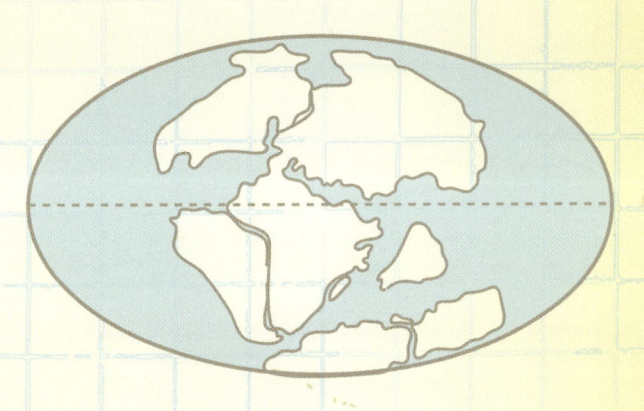

JURASSIC: 199- 145 million years ago

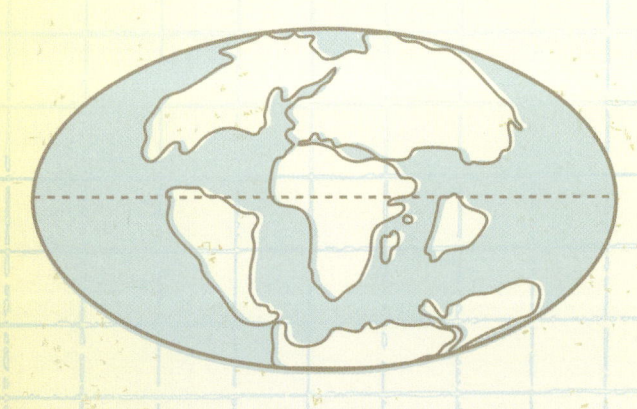

The Cretaceous

The continents began to look more like their current shape. By now, dinosaurs lived right across the globe – even at the north and south pole. They grew bigger and bigger.

CRETACEOUS: 145-66 million years ago

Before the dinosaurs

Dinosaurs were not always dominant. Before them, and in their earliest days, a number of predatory dinosaur-like and crocodile-like groups existed, as well as some mammal-like reptiles.

Archosaurs are a group of animals including dinosaurs, crocodiles, birds and pterosaurs. Primitive archosaurs like this one walked more like crocodiles.

The meteor that struck Earth is thought to have been about 15km wide – that's about the size of Manhattan Island in New York.

Extinction

So where did the dinosaurs go? Around 66 million years ago, a meteor struck the Earth, throwing huge clouds of gas into the atmosphere. Combined with large-scale volcanic eruptions, this dramatically changed temperatures around the world. Around three-quarters of all plants and animals went extinct.

Golden eagle

Extinct or evolved?

While many of the dinosaurs went extinct, some survived the chaos. They were a special line of dinosaurs – the birds. Able to adapt to the changing environments, they not only came out of the extinction event, but went on to flourish. Over time they evolved into the huge number of species we see around us today.

Ever seen a dinosaur?
Wait, so dinosaurs are still around today? Yes! Every bird you know, from a pigeon to an emu to a penguin, is technically a living, breathing dinosaur!

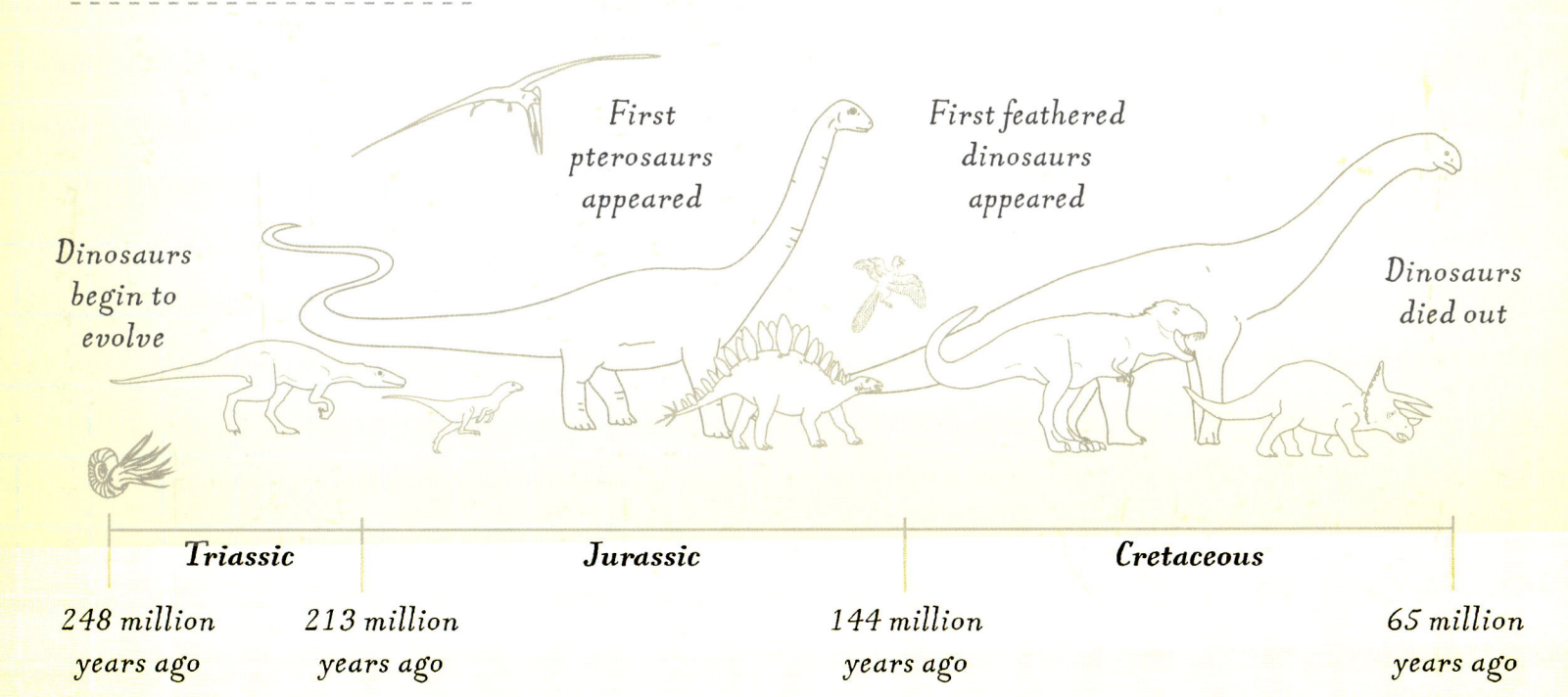

Dinosaur timeline

Dinosaurs begin to evolve

First pterosaurs appeared

First feathered dinosaurs appeared

Dinosaurs died out

| Triassic | | Jurassic | Cretaceous |

248 million years ago   213 million years ago   144 million years ago   65 million years ago

Dinosaurs Today

Almost everything we know about dinosaurs comes from studying their remains, known as fossils. Preserved over millions of years, fossils are usually made up of the hard part of an animal's body, such as its bones. The oldest fossils we know of are around 3.5 billion years old! They comprise the earliest forms of simple life, similar to bacteria.

What is a fossil?

The process of fossilisation takes many thousands of years to complete. It is a gradual process where the parts of an organism are slowly replaced with harder minerals, which can survive for millions of years. Scientists who study fossils are called palaeontologists.

Fantastic beasts

Before people understood what dinosaurs were, ancient cultures thought they were mythical creatures like dragons!

Often, when a dinosaur died it was washed into a lake or river. Here, its body was covered with water.

Next, its body decayed and rotted away. Usually just the skeleton remained.

Over very long periods of time, the skeleton was then covered with layers of sediment.

Over even longer periods of time, the sediment turned into rock, and the bones hardened. They transformed into fossils.

As the rocks erode away, the fossils are exposed again after millions of years. Now they can be excavated!

Trace fossils

Not all fossils are the preserved remains of a dead animal. Sometimes, we are lucky and find evidence of what a dinosaur was doing while it was alive. These are called trace fossils, and are useful evidence of dinosaur behaviour. Trace fossils include eggs, trackways and even fossilised faeces (poo).

Poo-ey!
Fossilised faeces are known as coprolites. They enable palaeontologists to work out what dinosaurs ate.

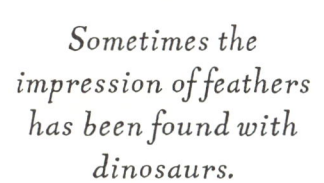

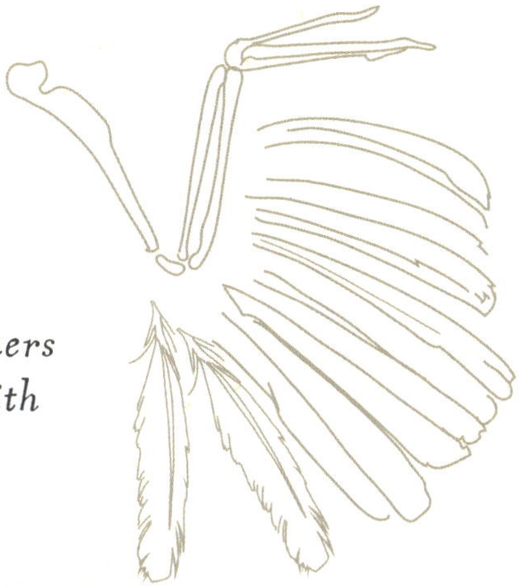

Sometimes the impression of feathers has been found with dinosaurs.

Fossil hunters

Researchers have also discovered fossilised wood, hair and resin (animals entombed in amber) – and even fossilised DNA. Palaeontologists are now able to examine these fossils with a range of modern high-tech scientific methods.

Most dinosaur bones are found as individual pieces, but sometimes a whole skull or even a skeleton is discovered!

A fossil ammonite – a type of mollusc that swam the ancient seas

Fossilised leaf impression

An ancient mosquito preserved in amber (fossilised tree resin)

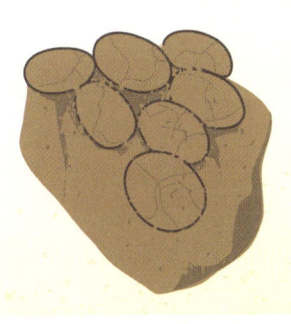

A clutch of ancient reptilian eggs

North America

Towards the end of the Jurassic, the super continent Pangaea quickly broke up, and the Atlantic Ocean separated North America from Africa and Europe. At this time, North America had a humid, tropical climate, with many different habitats. Later on, during the Cretaceous period, a shallow inland sea covered much of the centre of North America. The divide meant that distinct types of dinosaur evolved on either side of the water.

7

4

5

6

N
W E
S

Key

1. Brachiosaurus altithorax
2. Stegosaurus stenops
3. Archelon ischyros
4. Allosaurus fragilis
5. Dakotaraptor steini
6. Tyrannosaurus rex
7. Quetzalcoatlus northropi

Tyrannosaurus rex

Group: Theropod • Period: Cretaceous
Pronunciation: Tie-ran-oh-saw-rus rex

Tyrannosaurus rex was perhaps the largest carnivore ever to walk the Earth. It had one of the most powerful bites of any animal, with teeth like steak knives for tearing through flesh and crushing bone. Its name, meaning 'tyrant lizard king', reflects its spot at the top of the food chain in the Cretaceous period.

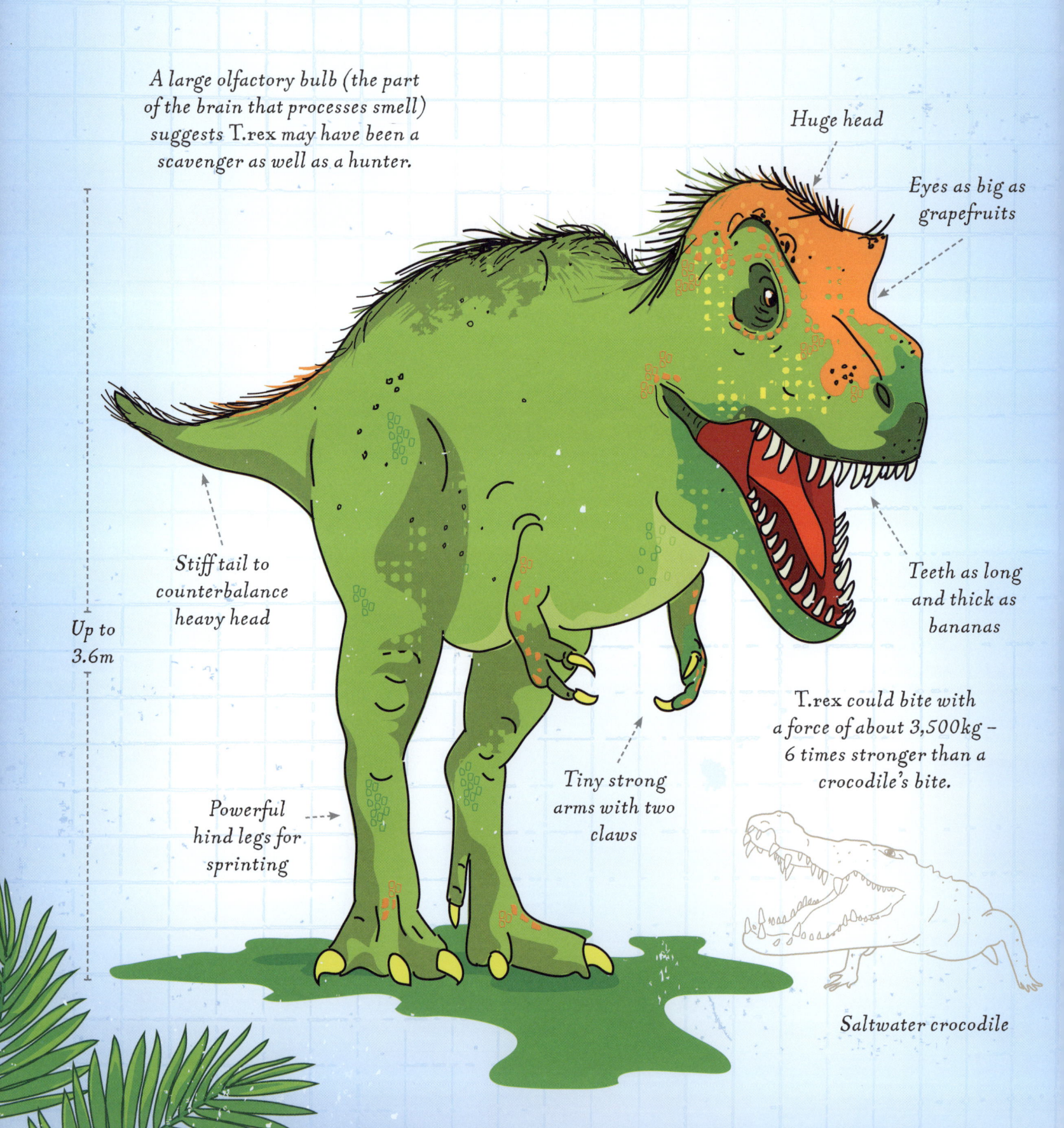

A large olfactory bulb (the part of the brain that processes smell) suggests T.rex may have been a scavenger as well as a hunter.

Huge head

Eyes as big as grapefruits

Teeth as long and thick as bananas

Stiff tail to counterbalance heavy head

Up to 3.6m

T.rex could bite with a force of about 3,500kg – 6 times stronger than a crocodile's bite.

Powerful hind legs for sprinting

Tiny strong arms with two claws

Saltwater crocodile

Allosaurus fragilis

Group: Theropod • Period: Jurassic
Pronunciation: Al-oh-saw-rus fra-jil-is

Often termed the 'wolf of the Jurassic', *Allosaurus* was among the top predators of its time. Packs of these fearsome hunters would chase after their prey, slowly draining their target of energy before diving in for the kill. Discovered in 1877, *Allosaurus* was one of the first dinosaur fossils discovered in North America.

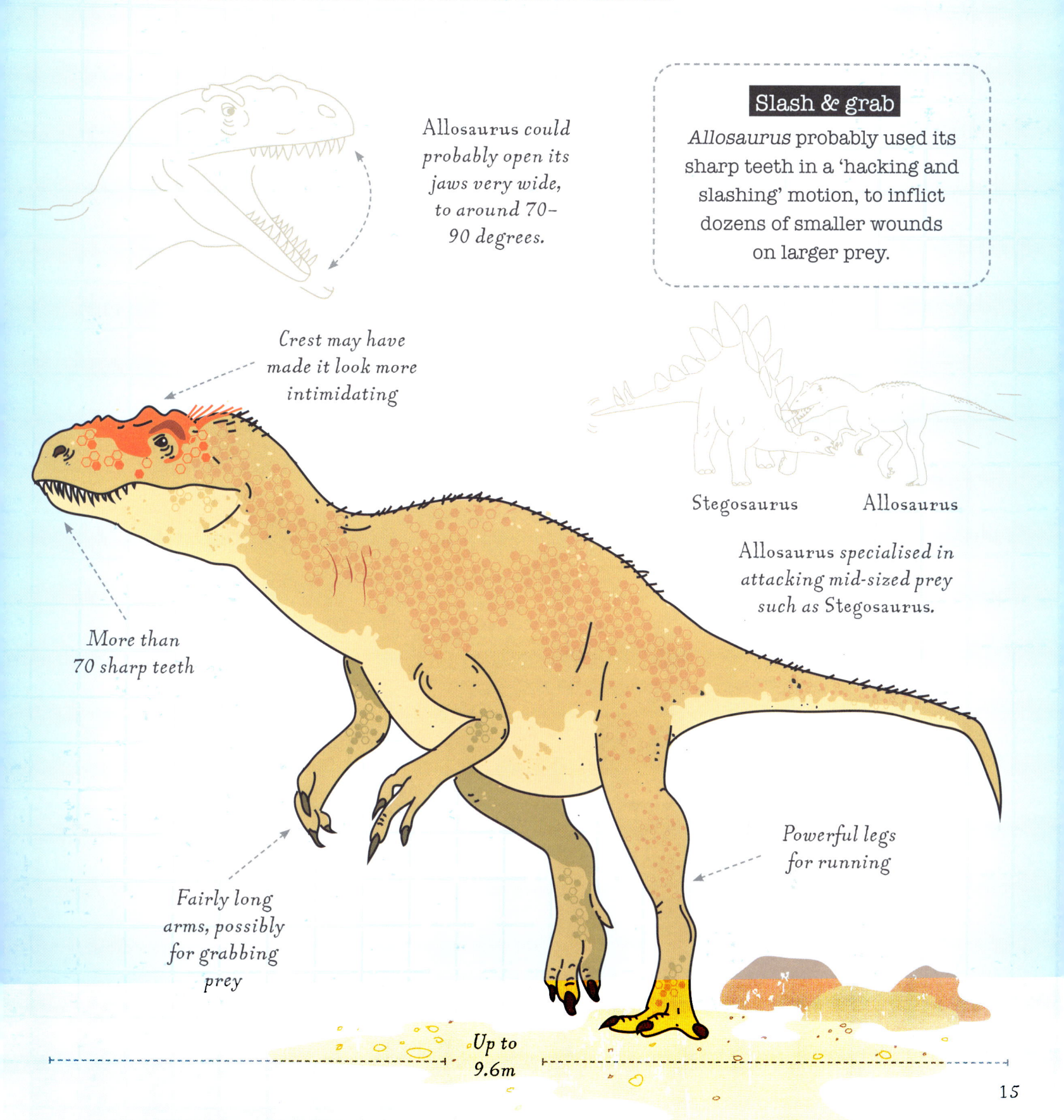

Allosaurus could probably open its jaws very wide, to around 70–90 degrees.

Slash & grab

Allosaurus probably used its sharp teeth in a 'hacking and slashing' motion, to inflict dozens of smaller wounds on larger prey.

Crest may have made it look more intimidating

Stegosaurus   Allosaurus

Allosaurus specialised in attacking mid-sized prey such as Stegosaurus.

More than 70 sharp teeth

Powerful legs for running

Fairly long arms, possibly for grabbing prey

Up to 9.6m

Dakotaraptor steini

Group: Theropod • Period: Cretaceous
Pronunciation: Da-koh-ta-rap-tor sty-nee

Dakotaraptor was the biggest of the theropods known as 'raptors' – slender, medium-sized hunters. Discovered in 2015, fossils revealed that it had feathered arms like the wings of modern birds, though it could not fly. This pack animal used its agility to capture prey before killing it with the huge sickle-shaped claws on its feet.

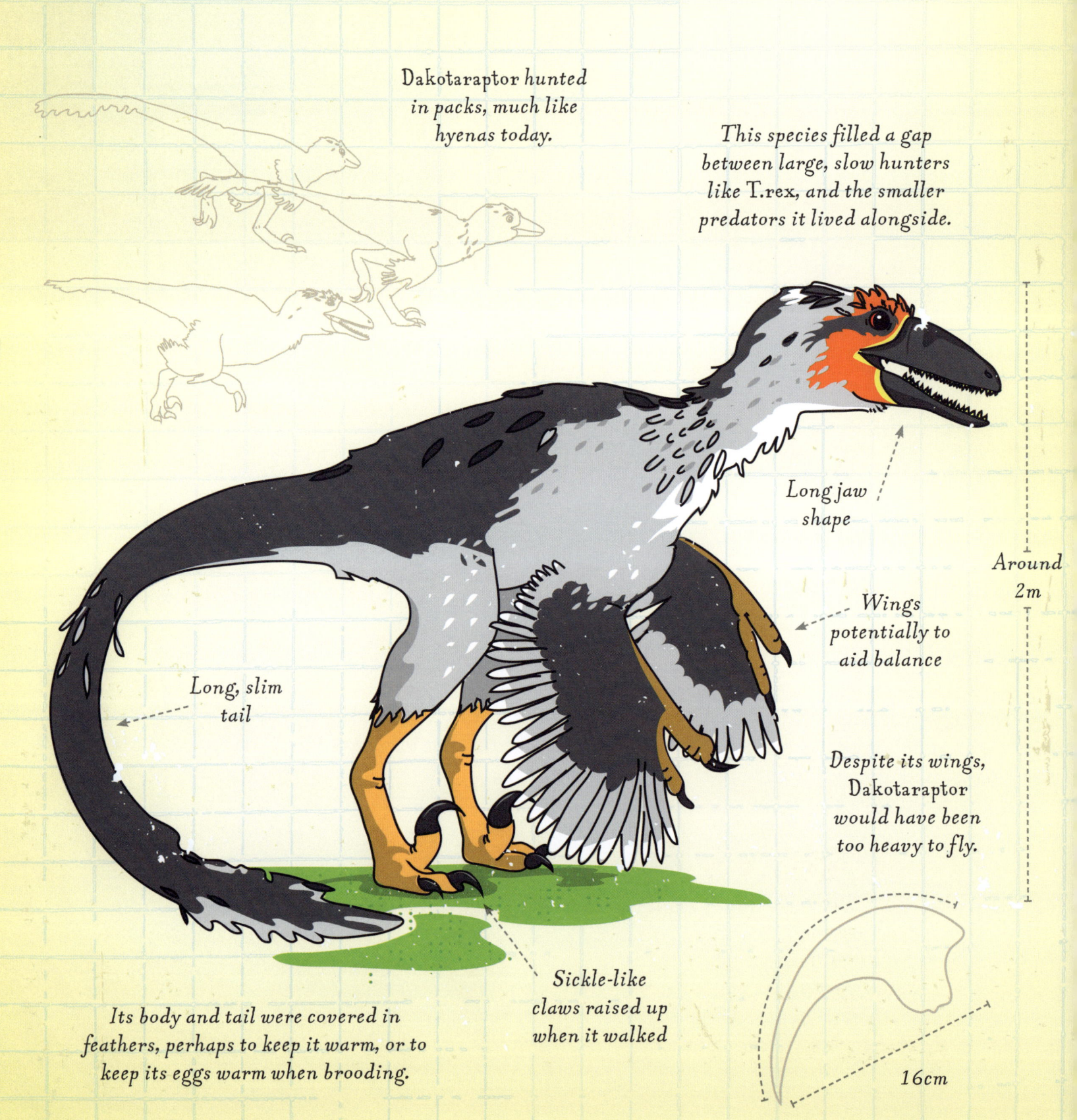

Dakotaraptor hunted in packs, much like hyenas today.

This species filled a gap between large, slow hunters like T.rex, and the smaller predators it lived alongside.

Long jaw shape

Around 2m

Wings potentially to aid balance

Long, slim tail

Despite its wings, Dakotaraptor would have been too heavy to fly.

Its body and tail were covered in feathers, perhaps to keep it warm, or to keep its eggs warm when brooding.

Sickle-like claws raised up when it walked

16cm

16

Troodon formosus

Group: Theropod • **Period:** Cretaceous
Pronunciation: Tru-don for-moh-sus

From studies of its skull and braincase (cranium), *Troodon* is possibly the most intelligent dinosaur known to us. It is thought to have hunted at night, and had large eyes for excellent vision in the dark. Serrated teeth and U-shaped jaws suggest *Troodon* was an omnivore, likely feeding on small animals, insects and perhaps plants.

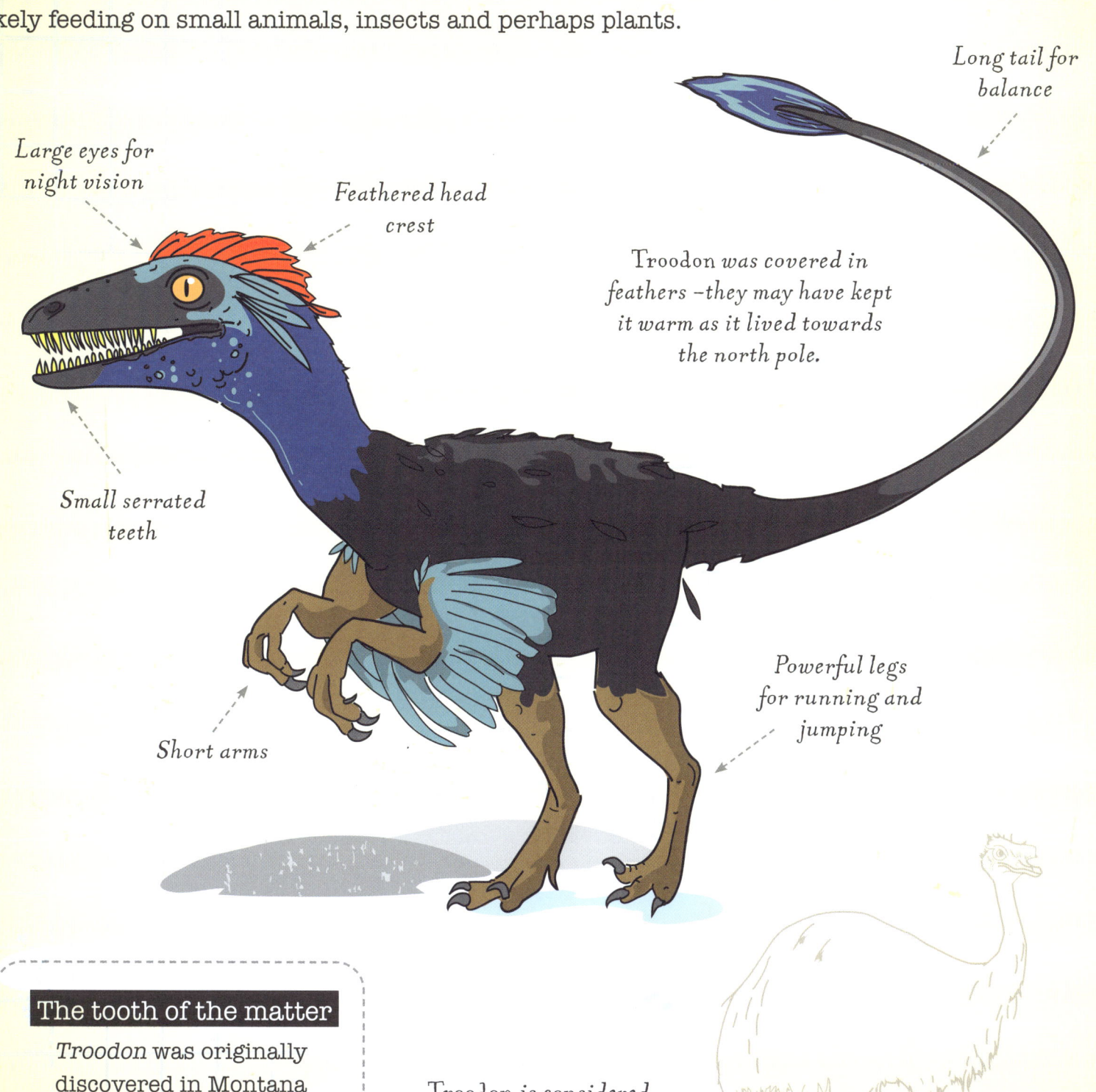

Long tail for balance

Large eyes for night vision

Feathered head crest

Troodon was covered in feathers – they may have kept it warm as it lived towards the north pole.

Small serrated teeth

Short arms

Powerful legs for running and jumping

Ostrich

The tooth of the matter

Troodon was originally discovered in Montana in 1856 and was named from just a single tooth. More of the skeleton has since been found.

Troodon is considered to be one of the smartest dinosaurs – it was probably as smart as large birds today.

17

Brachiosaurus altithorax

Group: Sauropod • Period: Jurassic
Pronunciation: Bra-kio-saw-rus al-tee-thor-ax

With its long neck, tiny head and bulky body, *Brachiosaurus* was fairly typical of a sauropod, except for its long front legs, which gave it an unusually upright stance. As it lived alongside other sauropods, this gave *Brachiosaurus* the advantage of being able to strip foliage away from the highest plants.

Around 9 m

Curved teeth

Mistaken identity

Brachiosaurus was originally identified based on fossils from Africa, but researchers later realised they were looking at two species: *Brachiosaurus* and *Giraffatitan*.

Air sacs in spine reduced weight

6 m

A single Brachiosaurus weighed around the same as about 20 African elephants.

Rear legs shorter than front legs

Brachiosaurus laid some of the biggest eggs ever at around 30cm long.

30cm

18

Diplodocus carnegii

Group: Sauropod • Period: Jurassic
Pronunciation: Dip-loh-doh-cus car-neg-ee-eye

A giant with a long neck and tail, *Diplodocus* is one of the best-known dinosaur species in the world. It probably achieved its huge size as part of an 'arms race' for defence against increasingly large and deadly predators such as *Allosaurus*. To maintain such enormous proportions, it had to spend most of its day eating and digesting.

Diplodocus would have had efficient lungs and a large, powerful heart to pump blood all the way up its long neck.

Around 30m

Diplodocus was as long as three buses.

Peg-like teeth

Ginkgo leaves

It would eat ginkgo plants by stripping leaves from their branches.

Swooping neck for reaching food

Cracking its whip-like tail could create a sonic boom to scare off predators.

Parasaurolophus walkeri

Group: Ornithopod • Period: Cretaceous
Pronunciation: Para-saw-rol-o-phus wal-ker-eye

Parasaurolophus was a large plant-eating dinosaur, easily recognised by the huge, quiff-like crest projecting from the back of its skull – the reason for its nickname 'Elvis' in the *Jurassic Park* movies. It probably used this crest to call other members of its species, or perhaps for display during courtship rituals.

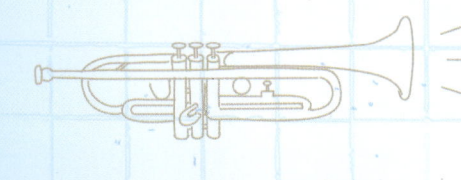

Parasaurolophus would have been the prey of choice for predators like T. rex.

Hollow head crest for signalling to mates or predators

Horn or snorkel?

Palaeontologists used to think that *Parasaurolophus* used its hollow head crest as a snorkel for swimming. Nowadays, most scientists think it was probably used like a trumpet to make a loud noise.

Hundreds of teeth grouped in sets called 'batteries'

Up to 4.9m

Walking

Running

Parasaurolophus could walk on four legs, or run on two.

Stegosaurus stenops

Group: Ornithopod • Period: Jurassic
Pronunciation: Ste-goh-saw-rus sten-ops

The tall, flat plates that grew down the back of this plant-eater would have been handy as armour, and may have helped the animal regulate its body temperature – soaking up warmth on cold days or releasing excess heat on warm ones. *Stegosaurus* also had huge, sharp spikes on its tail, which it could have swung at any predator that got too close.

What's in a name?
The name *Stegosaurus* comes from the Greek meaning 'roof lizard'. This refers to the armoured plates that ran down the top of the dinosaur's back.

Stegosaurus would have used its tail spikes as a weapon to fight off predators.

Plates up to 60cm tall and possibly brightly coloured

22 flat plates arranged in two rows

Brain the size of a walnut

Four tail spikes called 'thagomizers'

Stegosaurus walked slowly on all-fours.

Around 6m

21

Zuul crurivastator

Group: Ornithopod • Period: Cretaceous
Pronunciation: Zoo-ul crew-ree-vast-ate-or

Zuul was the first armoured dinosaur to be discovered with a complete tail club and skull. Built like a tank, it weighed around 2.5 tonnes. Its skull and back were covered in a shield of bony studs called osteoderms. These would have given it great protection against the predators of the time.

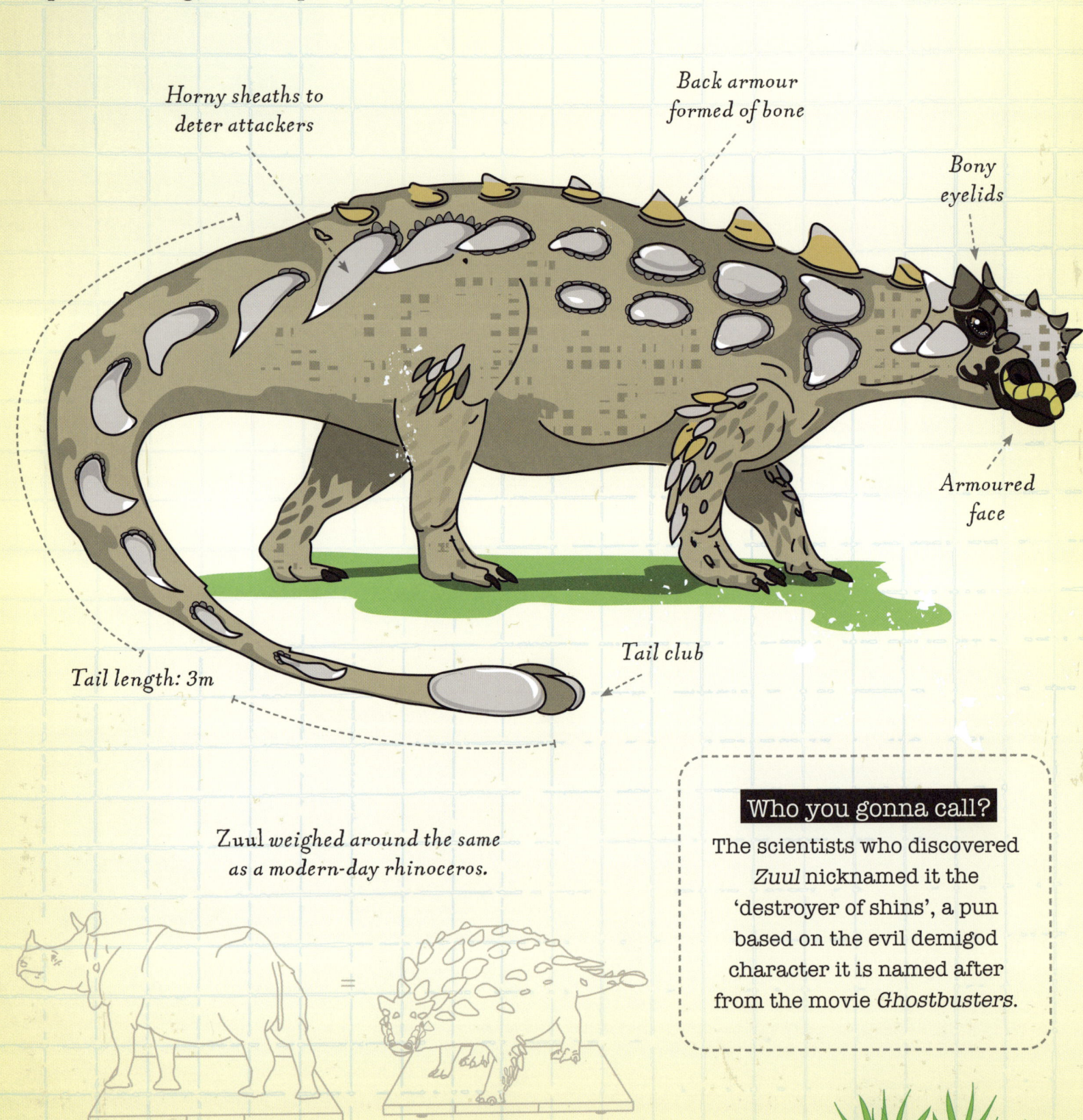

Horny sheaths to deter attackers

Back armour formed of bone

Bony eyelids

Armoured face

Tail length: 3m

Tail club

Zuul weighed around the same as a modern-day rhinoceros.

Rhinoceros = Zuul

Who you gonna call?
The scientists who discovered *Zuul* nicknamed it the 'destroyer of shins', a pun based on the evil demigod character it is named after from the movie *Ghostbusters*.

Triceratops horridus

Group: Ornithopod • **Period:** Cretaceous
Pronunciation: Tri-sera-tops hor-id-us

The name *Triceratops* means 'three-horned', referring to the three prominent horns on its face. These would have been used to protect it from predators such as *T.rex*, or to fight rival *Triceratops*. Like modern elephants and rhinos, *Triceratops* probably moved about in herds for protection, so scientists think it was a social animal.

Triceratops was about the same size as a modern African elephant.

African elephant   Triceratops

Two horns on forehead

Horn length: 1.15m

Neck frill for defence or displays

Short horn

Round, heavy body

Beak for stripping plant matter

Triceratops would have eaten woody plants such as cycads, which had cone-like seeds and evergreen leaves.

Pachycephalosaurus wyomingensis

Group: Ornithopod • Period: Cretaceous
Pronunciation: Pak-ee-cef-alo-saw-rus wyo-ming-en-sis

Easily identified by its thick, domed skull, *Pachycephalosaurus* was a small plant-eating dinosaur that lived towards the Cretaceous period. It used its huge, heavy head as a weapon, to fend off predators, or for combat with other members of its species.

Like modern deer, Pachycephalosaurs probably fought each other for territory or mates.

Rivals may have aimed for each other's flanks (sides), like giraffes do today.

The skull bone was up to 24cm thick – 20 times thicker than other dinosaur skulls!

Bony spikes around head

Domed skull

Beak full of leaf-shaped teeth

Relatively long legs and tail for quick running

Around 6m

Quetzalcoatlus northropi

Group: Pterosaur • Period: Cretaceous
Pronunciation: Kwet-zal-co-at-lus nor-throp-eye

Quetzalcoatlus was one of the largest flying animals of all time, with a wingspan of up to 15 metres. It ruled the skies during the time of the dinosaurs, alongside other pterosaurs (flying reptiles) and some of the first birds. It had a long, stiff neck, and a sharp, toothless beak, perfect for catching fish and other smaller prey, including dinosaurs.

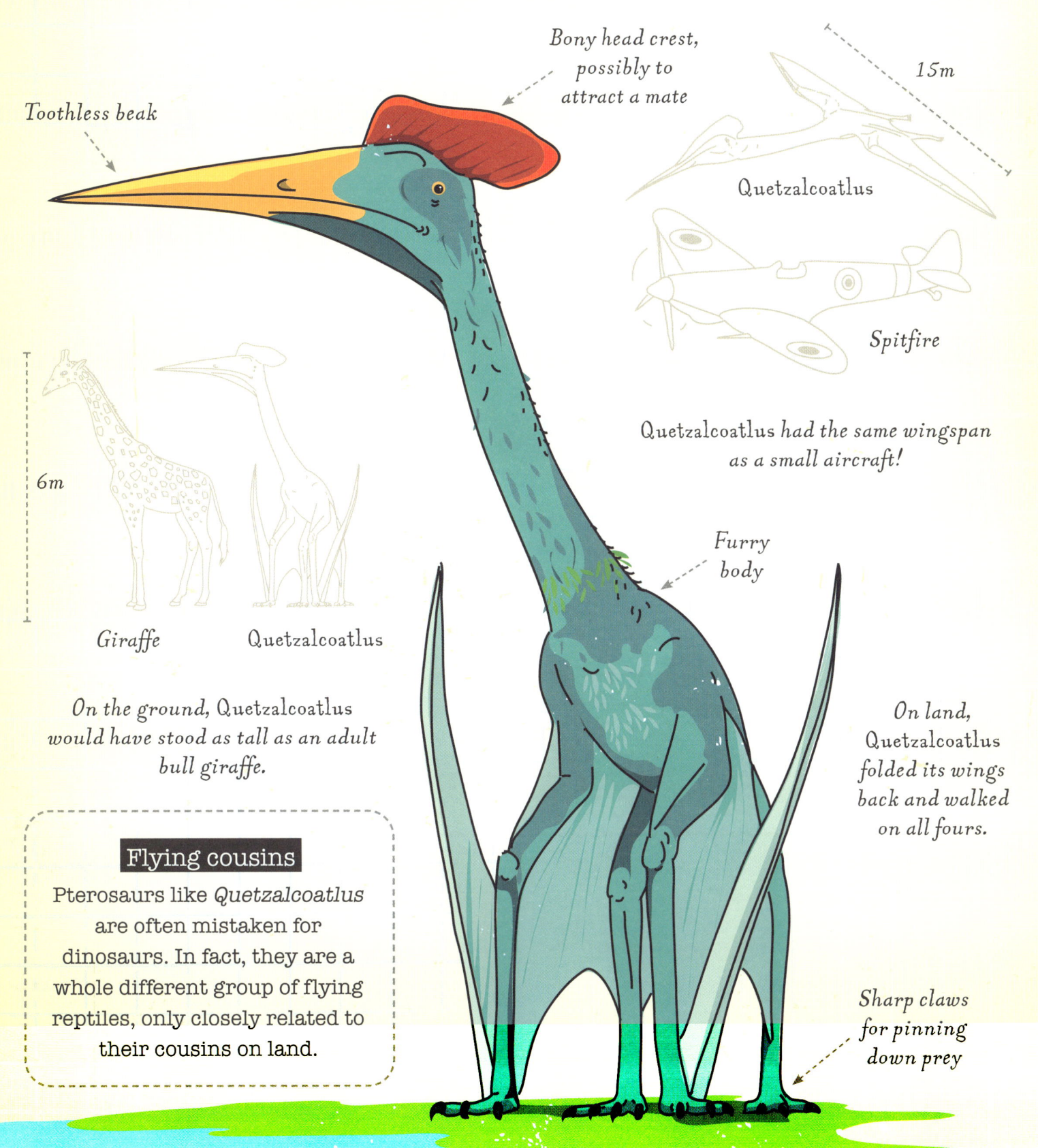

Toothless beak

Bony head crest, possibly to attract a mate

15m

Quetzalcoatlus

Spitfire

Quetzalcoatlus had the same wingspan as a small aircraft!

6m

Giraffe   Quetzalcoatlus

On the ground, Quetzalcoatlus would have stood as tall as an adult bull giraffe.

Furry body

On land, Quetzalcoatlus folded its wings back and walked on all fours.

Flying cousins

Pterosaurs like *Quetzalcoatlus* are often mistaken for dinosaurs. In fact, they are a whole different group of flying reptiles, only closely related to their cousins on land.

Sharp claws for pinning down prey

25

Archelon ischyros

Group: Prehistoric turtles • Period: Cretaceous
Pronunciation: Ar-kel-on ish-eye-ros

Archelon is the largest sea turtle that ever existed – the biggest specimen ever found was 4 metres in length and 5 metres wide from flipper to flipper. *Archelon* swam the shallow seas that covered much of North America during the Cretaceous period.

Sharp beak for breaking open shells

Carapace (upper shell)

Pointed tail

Shell made of a bony framework beneath leathery plates

Archelon might have been able to retract its head and neck into its shell when threatened.

Around 4m

Probably an open ocean swimmer, Archelon could have covered long distances each day.

Big flippers

Archelon

Archelon was around three times larger than the biggest turtles today.

Leatherback turtle

Tylosaurus proriger

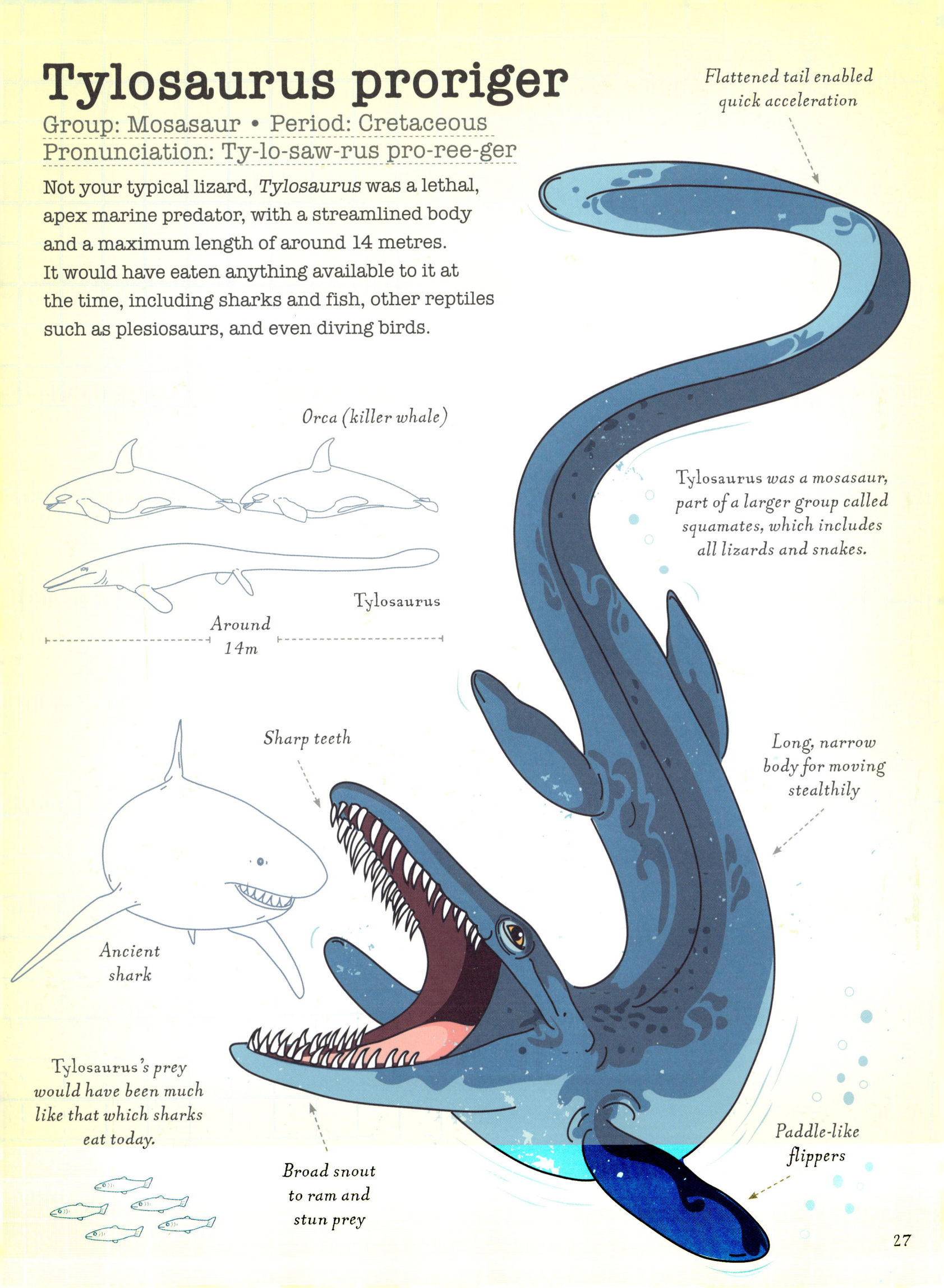

Group: Mosasaur • Period: Cretaceous
Pronunciation: Ty-lo-saw-rus pro-ree-ger

Not your typical lizard, *Tylosaurus* was a lethal, apex marine predator, with a streamlined body and a maximum length of around 14 metres. It would have eaten anything available to it at the time, including sharks and fish, other reptiles such as plesiosaurs, and even diving birds.

Flattened tail enabled quick acceleration

Orca (killer whale)

Tylosaurus

Around 14m

Tylosaurus was a mosasaur, part of a larger group called squamates, which includes all lizards and snakes.

Sharp teeth

Ancient shark

Tylosaurus's prey would have been much like that which sharks eat today.

Long, narrow body for moving stealthily

Broad snout to ram and stun prey

Paddle-like flippers

27

Key

1. Herrerasaurus ischigualastensis
2. Anhanguera bittersdorffi
3. Amargasaurus cazaui
4. Patagotitan mayorum
5. Carnotaurus sastrei
6. Dakosaurus andiniensis

South America

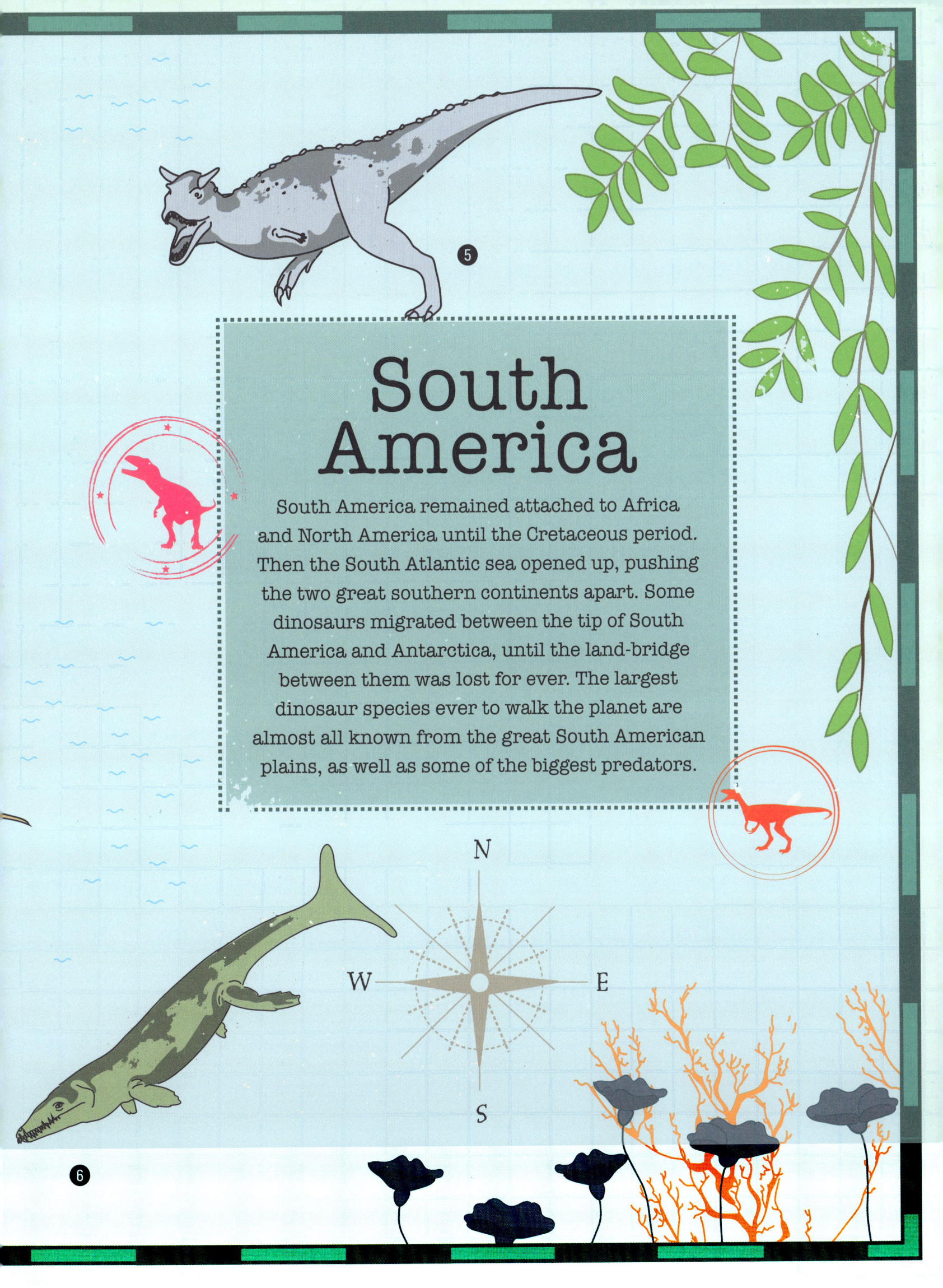

South America remained attached to Africa and North America until the Cretaceous period. Then the South Atlantic sea opened up, pushing the two great southern continents apart. Some dinosaurs migrated between the tip of South America and Antarctica, until the land-bridge between them was lost for ever. The largest dinosaur species ever to walk the planet are almost all known from the great South American plains, as well as some of the biggest predators.

Herrerasaurus ischigualastensis

Group: Theropod • Period: Triassic
Pronunciation: Herr-err-ah-sore-us iss-she-gwa-last-en-sis

Herrerasaurus was one of the very first dinosaurs, living around 230 million years ago. At this time, dinosaurs were not yet the dominant land animals. Many non-dinosaur reptiles prowled the land, and they were often larger and fiercer than *Herrerasaurus*. However, at 3 to 6 metres long, *Herrerasaurus* would still have been a lethal predator.

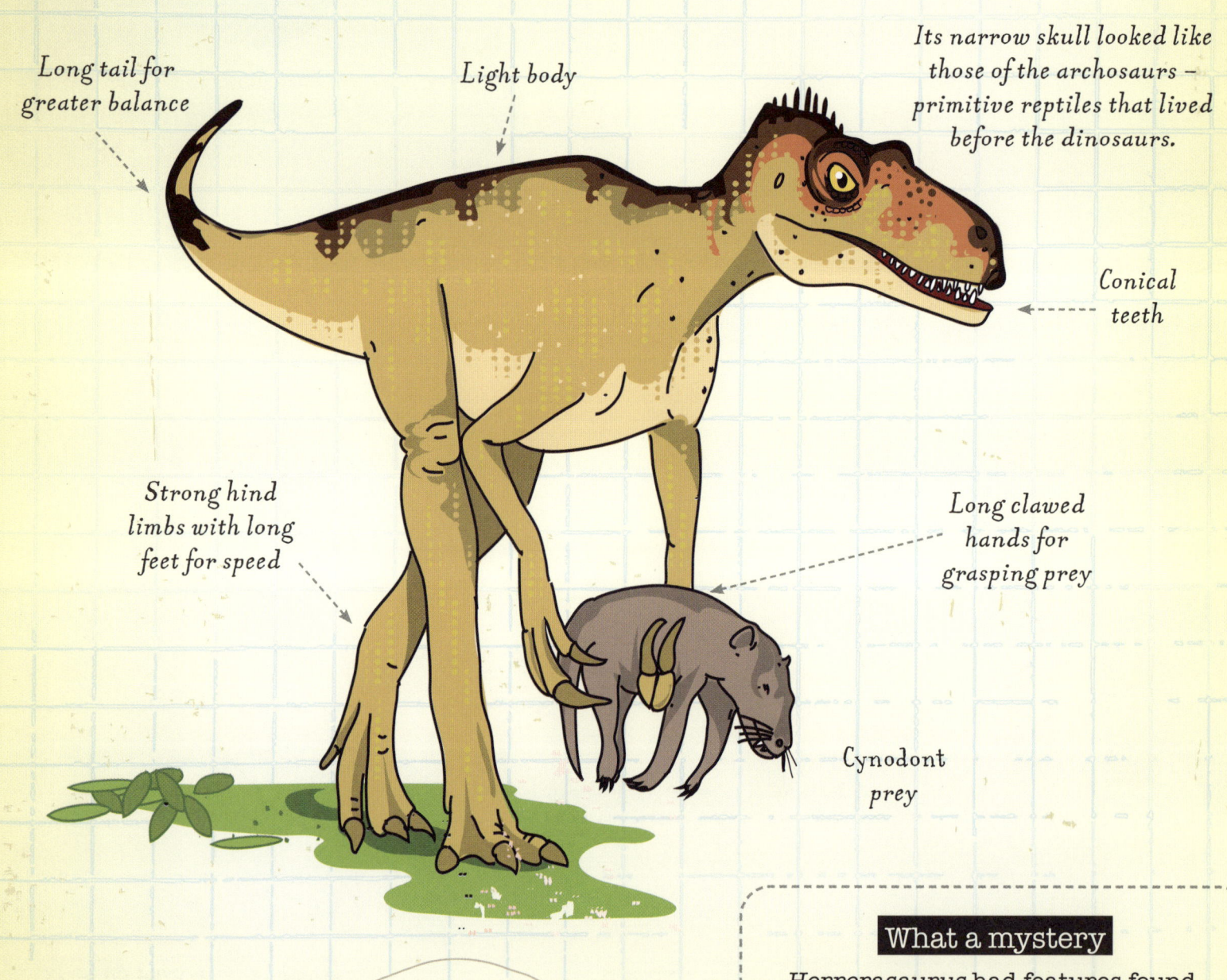

Long tail for greater balance

Light body

Its narrow skull looked like those of the archosaurs – primitive reptiles that lived before the dinosaurs.

Conical teeth

Strong hind limbs with long feet for speed

Long clawed hands for grasping prey

Cynodont prey

Herrerasaurus fed on mammal-like creatures such as cynodonts.

What a mystery

Herrerasaurus had features found in different groups of dinosaurs, and even non-dinosaurs. For many years, scientists did not know which group it belonged to. Then in 1988 a well-preserved skeleton was discovered, which revealed it was a theropod.

Giganotosaurus carolinii

Group: Theropod • Period: Cretaceous
Pronunciation: Jeye-gan-oh-toh-sore-us cah-roh-linn-ee

This huge carnivorous dinosaur may have grown even larger than *T.rex*, its counterpart in the northern hemisphere. It had a strong thick neck and a bulky skull filled with sharp teeth, perfect for tearing chunks of flesh off its victims. It was fast for its size too, capable of sprinting at speeds of up to 50 kilometres per hour.

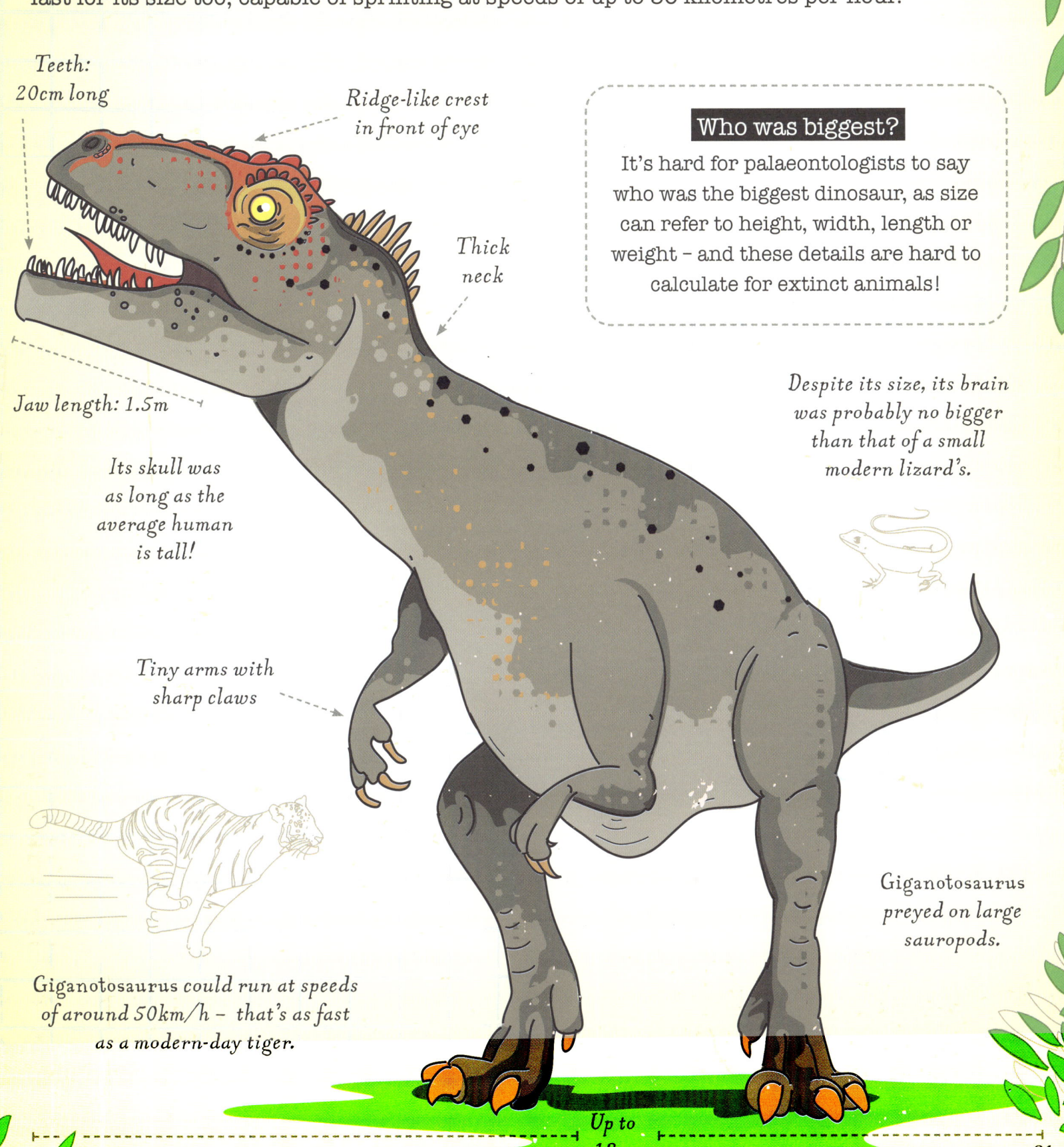

Teeth: 20cm long

Ridge-like crest in front of eye

Thick neck

Who was biggest?
It's hard for palaeontologists to say who was the biggest dinosaur, as size can refer to height, width, length or weight – and these details are hard to calculate for extinct animals!

Jaw length: 1.5m

Its skull was as long as the average human is tall!

Despite its size, its brain was probably no bigger than that of a small modern lizard's.

Tiny arms with sharp claws

Giganotosaurus preyed on large sauropods.

Giganotosaurus could run at speeds of around 50km/h – that's as fast as a modern-day tiger.

Up to 13m

Carnotaurus sastrei

Group: Theropod • Period: Cretaceous
Pronunciation: Car-noh-tore-us sass-tree-eye

The name *Carnotaurus* means 'meat-eating bull' in Latin, in reference to the unique bull-like horns above this dinosaur's eyes. It was a moderately-sized carnivore, with a short neck and even shorter arms. These tiny arms were functionally useless, similar to the wings of flightless birds such as emus and ostriches today.

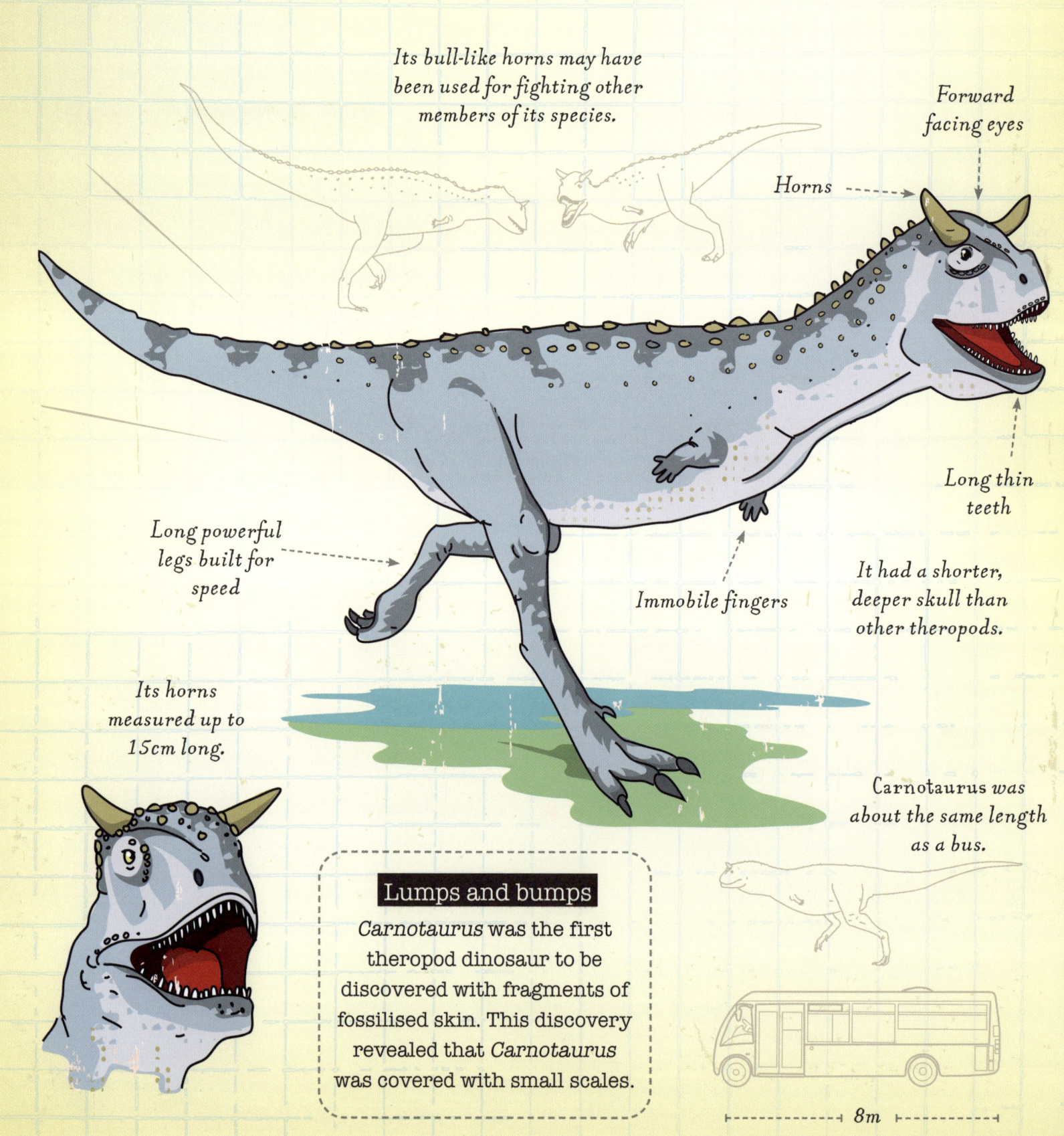

Its bull-like horns may have been used for fighting other members of its species.

Forward facing eyes

Horns

Long powerful legs built for speed

Long thin teeth

Immobile fingers

It had a shorter, deeper skull than other theropods.

Its horns measured up to 15cm long.

Carnotaurus was about the same length as a bus.

Lumps and bumps

Carnotaurus was the first theropod dinosaur to be discovered with fragments of fossilised skin. This discovery revealed that *Carnotaurus* was covered with small scales.

8m

Eoraptor lunensis

Group: Theropod • Period: Triassic
Pronunciation: Ee-oh-rap-tor loo-nen-sis

Eoraptor is considered by many to be the earliest dinosaur known to us. Small and lightly-built, it ran on its hindlimbs to catch prey and avoid larger predators. Unusually, it had several different types of teeth (a characteristic called 'heterodonty') suggesting that it had an omnivorous diet, consisting of plants and small animals.

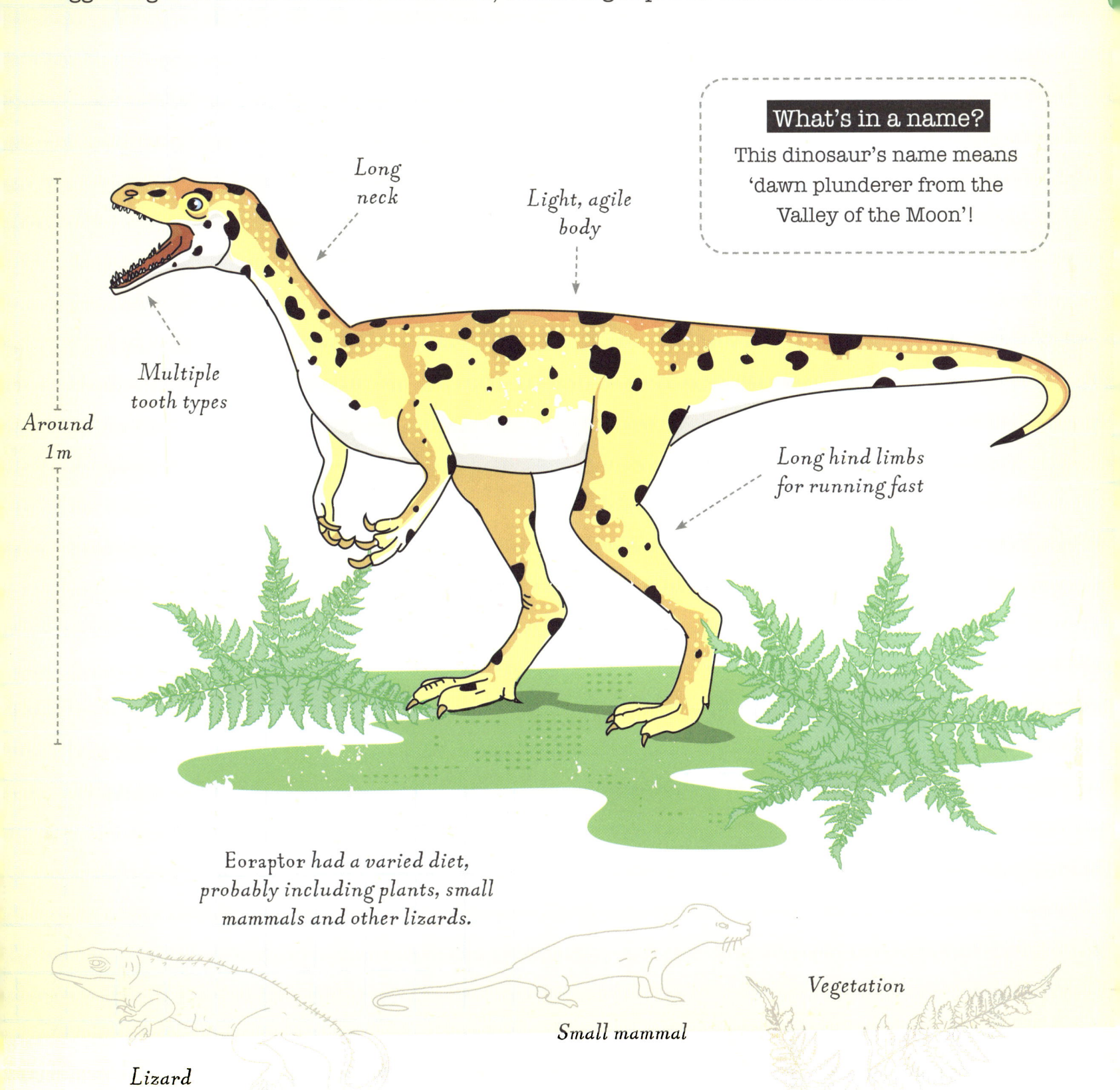

What's in a name?
This dinosaur's name means 'dawn plunderer from the Valley of the Moon'!

Long neck

Light, agile body

Multiple tooth types

Around 1m

Long hind limbs for running fast

Eoraptor *had a varied diet, probably including plants, small mammals and other lizards.*

Lizard

Small mammal

Vegetation

Patagotitan mayorum

Group: Sauropod • Period: Cretaceous
Pronunciation: Pah-tah-goh-tie-tan may-oar-rum

Patagotitan belonged to a group of sauropods called titanosaurs – all known for their enormous size. With around 130 bones discovered from 6 individuals, this is one of the better known species. A true giant, *Patagotitan* came in at around 37 metres in length and weighed up to 70 tonnes. This makes it one of the largest animals ever to have lived.

Small head and peg-shaped teeth

Boeing 757

37m

Patagotitan

The biggest land animal ever discovered, Patagotitan was about the length of a jet liner.

Neck longer than body

Hollow bones may have helped Patagotitan to breathe more efficiently.

Light and airy

Despite its size, *Patagotitan* did not weigh as much as some smaller dinosaurs. This was due to its hollow bones, which ensured it did not collapse under its sheer size.

Its thigh bone was the size of a sofa!

Amargasaurus cazaui

Group: Sauropod • Period: Cretaceous
Pronunciation: Am-ar-goh-sore-us caz-ow-eye

Relatively small for a sauropod, *Amargasaurus* was still around 10 metres long. Uniquely, it had a double row of bony spines projecting from its neck and back. The largest of these were around 60 centimetres in length. It is thought that they may have supported some sort of sail for protection or display.

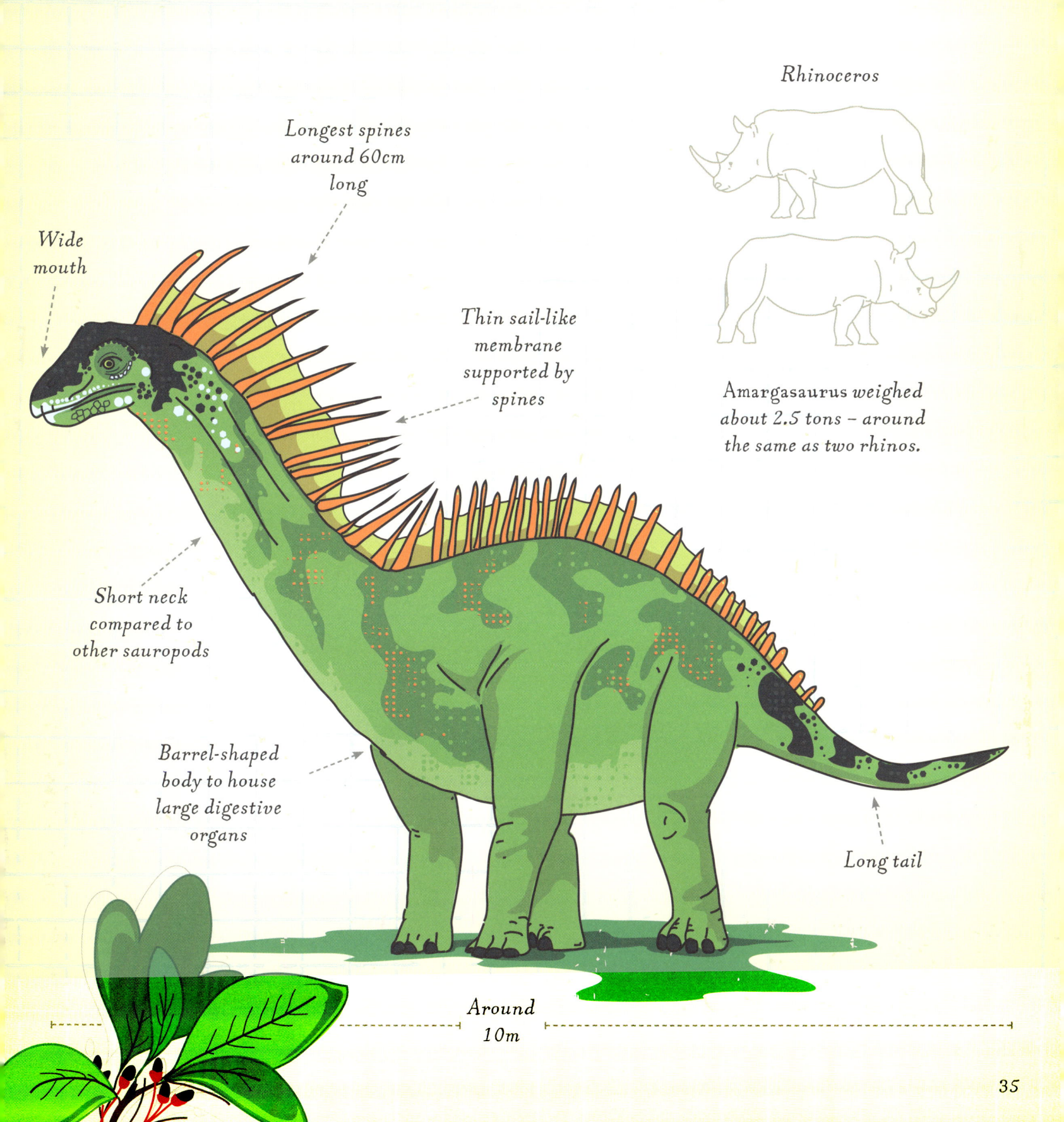

Longest spines around 60cm long

Rhinoceros

Wide mouth

Thin sail-like membrane supported by spines

Amargasaurus weighed about 2.5 tons – around the same as two rhinos.

Short neck compared to other sauropods

Barrel-shaped body to house large digestive organs

Long tail

Around 10m

Dreadnoughtus schrani

Group: Sauropod • **Period:** Cretaceous
Pronunciation: Dred-nought-us sh-ran-eye

Similar to *Patagotitan*, *Dreadnoughtus* was a member of the titanosaur family. It had an enormously long neck, making up nearly half of its total length and reaching the height of a 2-storey house. The biggest specimen of *Dreadnoughtus* found so far shows evidence that it was still growing at the time of its death – so there might be even bigger specimens out there waiting to be discovered!

What's in a name?
Dreadnoughtus, whose name means 'fears nothing', shares its name with the armoured battleships of the early 20th century.

Tyrannosaurus rex

Dreadnoughtus would have weighed more than five T.rexes. It was one of the biggest known land animals of all time.

Dreadnoughtus could have swung its long tail like a whip for defence against predators.

Broad shoulders

Long neck

Whip-like tail

The biggest specimen found was nearly as long as 7 cars.

Up to 26m

Talenkauen santacrucensis

Group: Ornithopod • Period: Cretaceous
Pronunciation: Tal-enk-ow-en san-tah-crew-en-sis

This small ornithischian had a series of bony, oval-shaped plates running along the side of its ribcage. These were only around 3 millimetres thick but might have been an adaptation to protect it from predators. It had some very primitive features, such as a beak with teeth in the tip, and an extra toe, which most ornithischians lost as they evolved.

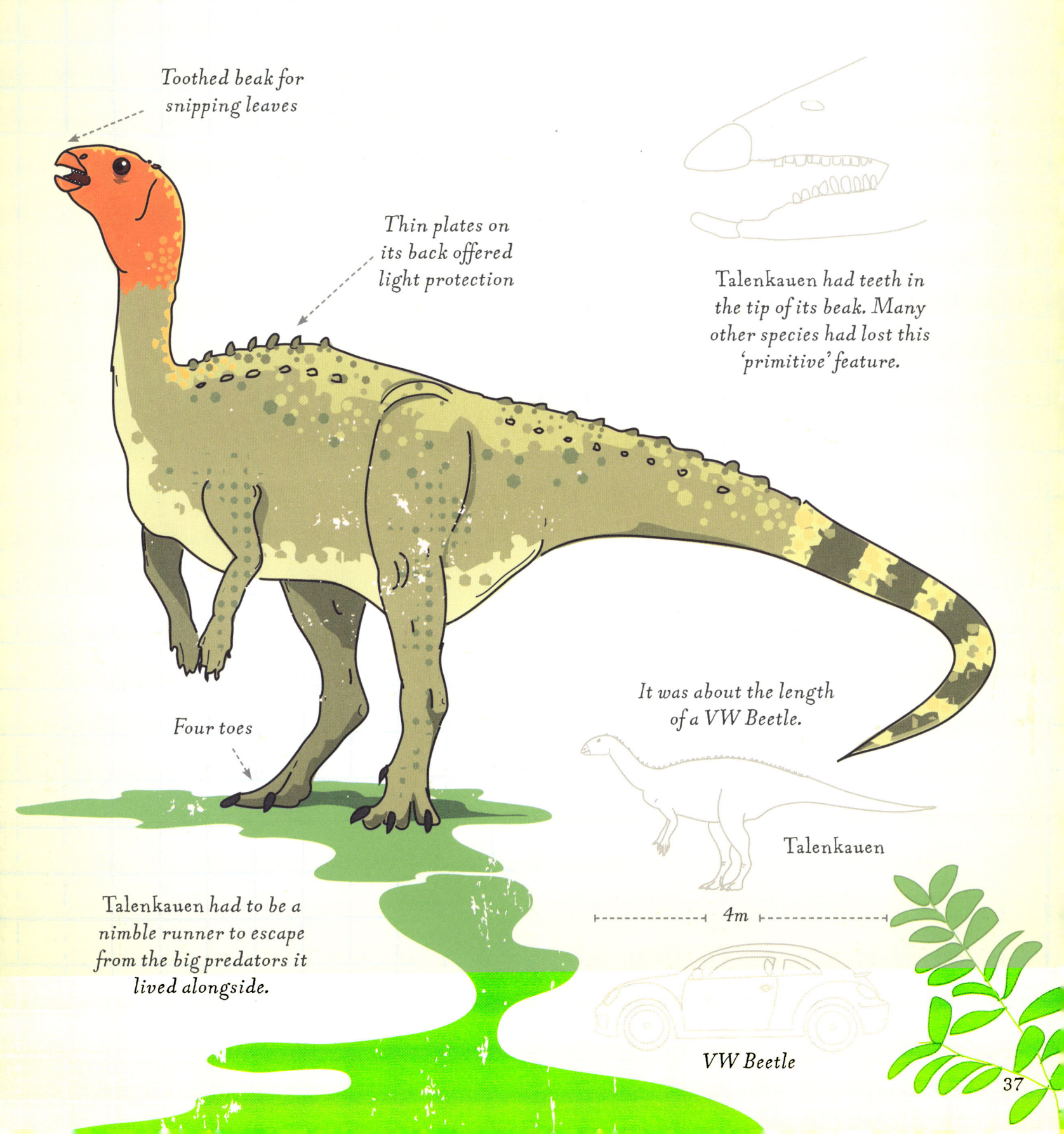

Toothed beak for snipping leaves

Thin plates on its back offered light protection

Talenkauen had teeth in the tip of its beak. Many other species had lost this 'primitive' feature.

Four toes

It was about the length of a VW Beetle.

Talenkauen

4m

Talenkauen *had to be a nimble runner to escape from the big predators it lived alongside.*

VW Beetle

37

Anhanguera blittersdorffi

Group: Pterosauria • Period: Cretaceous
Pronunciation: An-han-gwer-a blit-ters-dorf-fi

Anhanguera was an agile, medium-sized pterosaur with a wingspan of around 4.5 metres. At the tip of its jaws, it had strange, rounded crests full of sharp, conical teeth for spearing fish. Like other pterosaurs, its wings were made of a thin membrane of skin, stretched between its extremely long fingers.

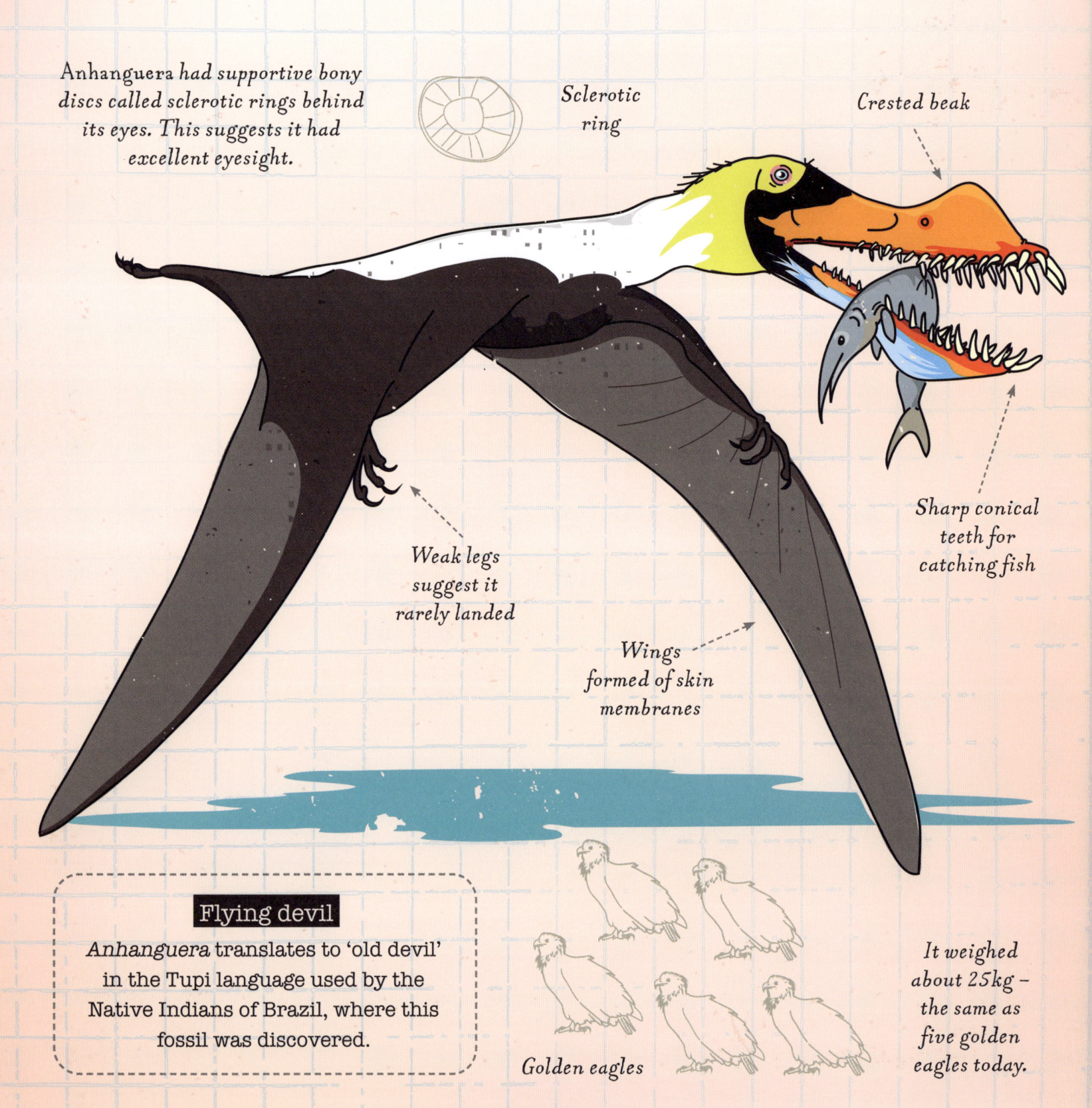

Anhanguera had supportive bony discs called sclerotic rings behind its eyes. This suggests it had excellent eyesight.

Sclerotic ring

Crested beak

Sharp conical teeth for catching fish

Weak legs suggest it rarely landed

Wings formed of skin membranes

Flying devil

Anhanguera translates to 'old devil' in the Tupi language used by the Native Indians of Brazil, where this fossil was discovered.

Golden eagles

It weighed about 25kg – the same as five golden eagles today.

Dakosaurus andiniensis

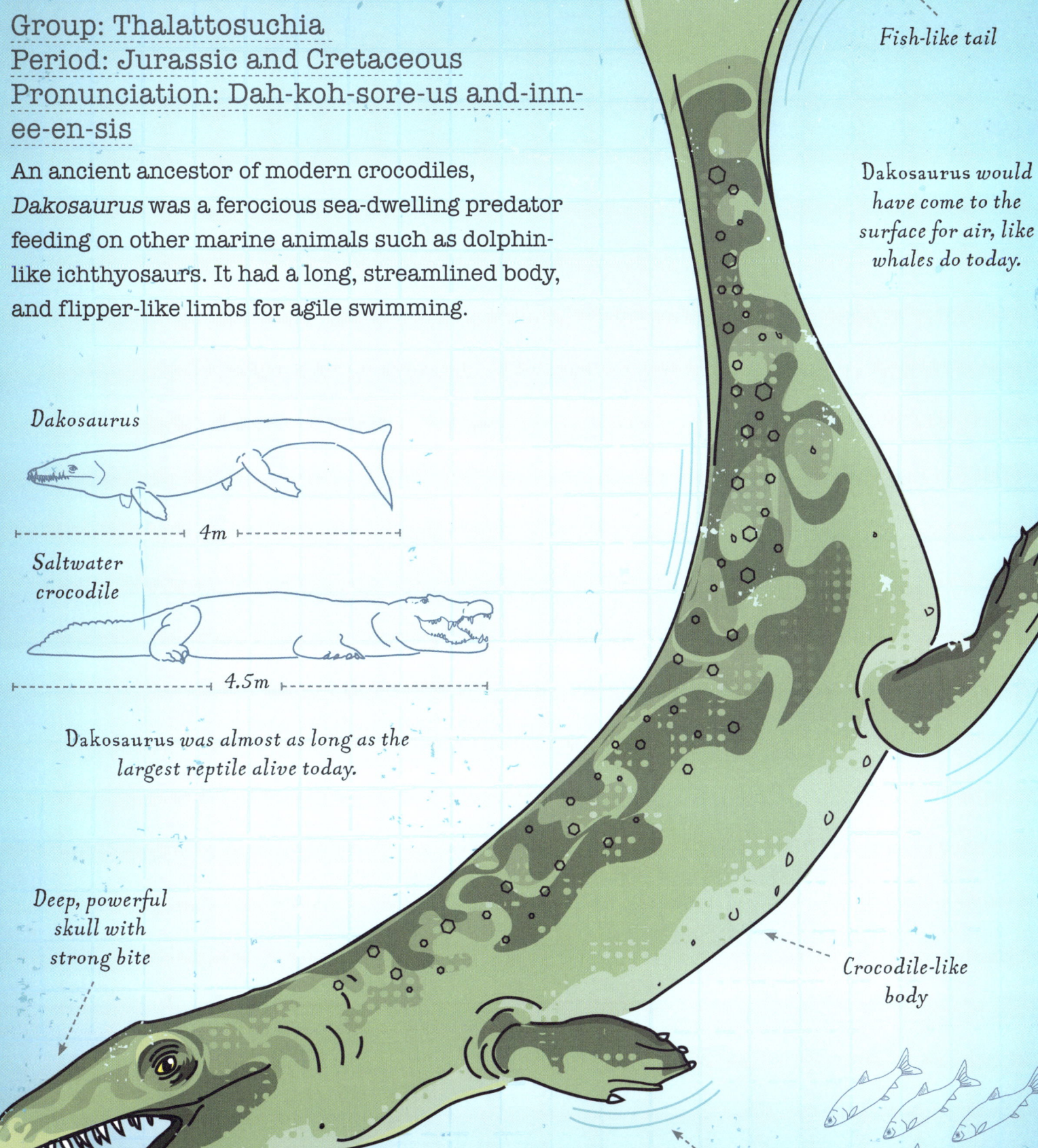

Group: Thalattosuchia
Period: Jurassic and Cretaceous
Pronunciation: Dah-koh-sore-us and-inn-ee-en-sis

An ancient ancestor of modern crocodiles, *Dakosaurus* was a ferocious sea-dwelling predator feeding on other marine animals such as dolphin-like ichthyosaurs. It had a long, streamlined body, and flipper-like limbs for agile swimming.

Dakosaurus
4m

Saltwater crocodile
4.5m

Dakosaurus was almost as long as the largest reptile alive today.

Deep, powerful skull with strong bite

Large teeth with serrated edges

Fish-like tail

Dakosaurus would have come to the surface for air, like whales do today.

Crocodile-like body

Turtle-like flippers

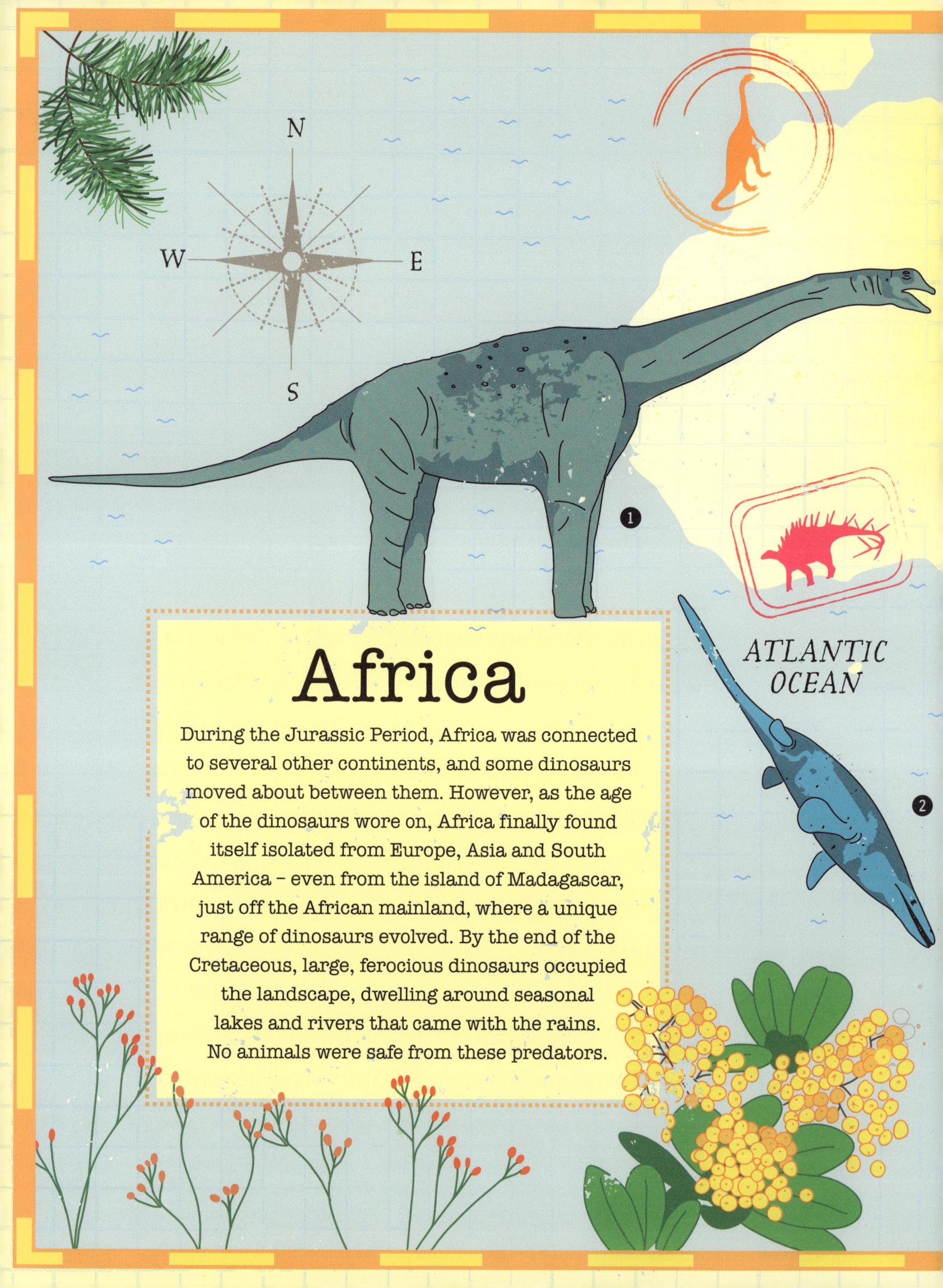

Africa

During the Jurassic Period, Africa was connected to several other continents, and some dinosaurs moved about between them. However, as the age of the dinosaurs wore on, Africa finally found itself isolated from Europe, Asia and South America – even from the island of Madagascar, just off the African mainland, where a unique range of dinosaurs evolved. By the end of the Cretaceous, large, ferocious dinosaurs occupied the landscape, dwelling around seasonal lakes and rivers that came with the rains. No animals were safe from these predators.

ATLANTIC OCEAN

Key

1. Paralititan stromeri
2. Angolasaurus bocagei
3. Carcharodontosaurus saharicus
4. Lesothosaurus diagnosticus
5. Alcione elainus
6. Spinosaurus aegyptiacus

INDIAN OCEAN

Spinosaurus aegyptiacus

Group: Theropod • Period: Cretaceous
Pronunciation: Spy-no-sore-us ay-jip-tee-ack-us

Spinosaurus was an enormous predator with a tall sail running down its back. Its sail alone was nearly as tall as a human, and may have flushed red to attract potential mates or to help regulate temperature. Its other features were like those of a crocodile, with curved claws, sharp teeth for skewering prey and expert fishing skills.

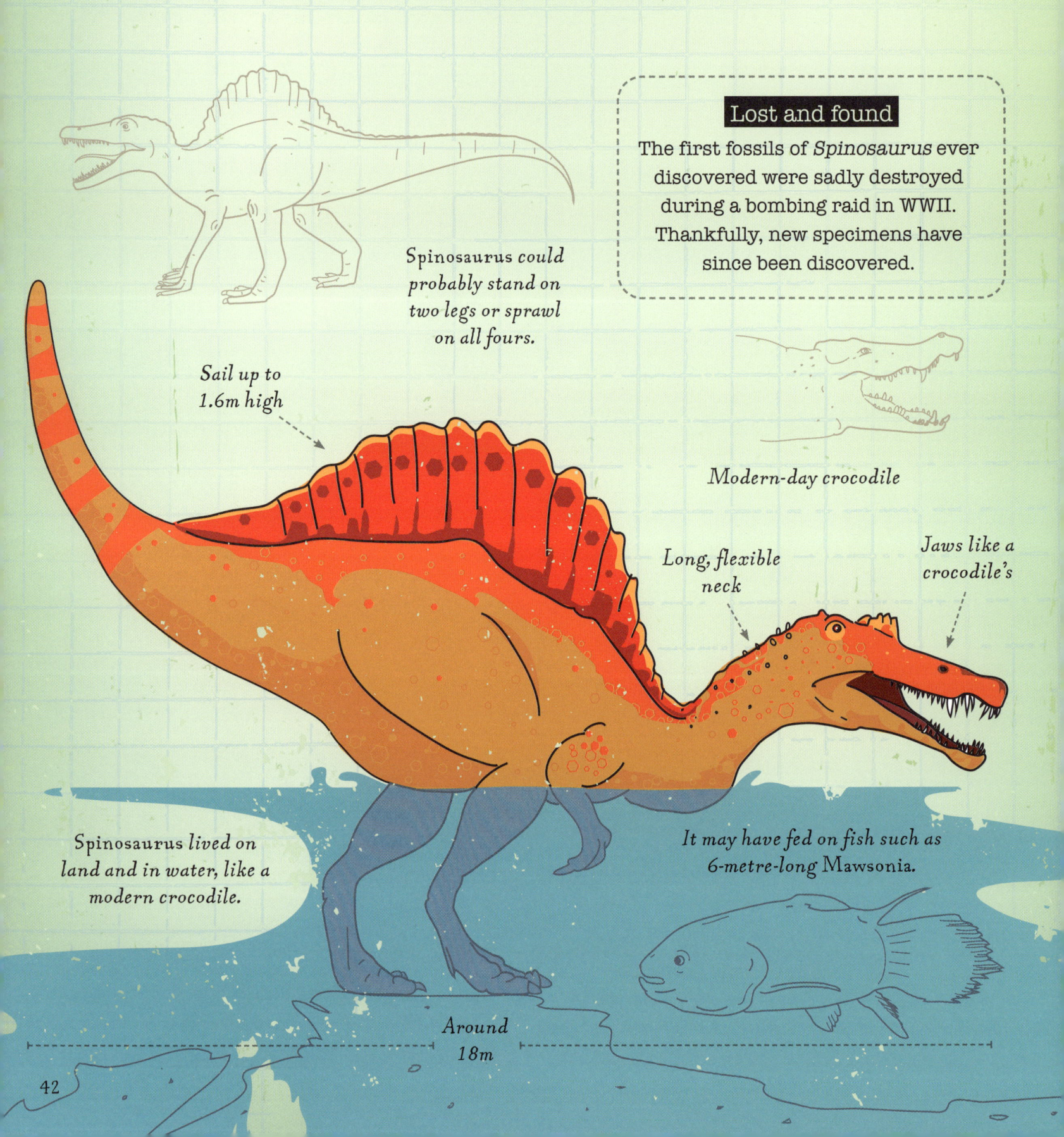

Spinosaurus could probably stand on two legs or sprawl on all fours.

Lost and found

The first fossils of *Spinosaurus* ever discovered were sadly destroyed during a bombing raid in WWII. Thankfully, new specimens have since been discovered.

Sail up to 1.6m high

Modern-day crocodile

Long, flexible neck

Jaws like a crocodile's

Spinosaurus lived on land and in water, like a modern crocodile.

It may have fed on fish such as 6-metre-long Mawsonia.

Around 18m

Carcharodontosaurus saharicus

Group: Theropod • Period: Cretaceous
Pronunciation: Kar-car-oh-don-toe-sor-us sa-ha-rik-us

First discovered in the deserts of Algeria and Egypt, *Carcharodontosaurus* was one of the most fearsome predators of North Africa. At around 14 metres long, it was possibly even bigger than North America's *T. rex* and South America's *Giganotosaurus*! Like them, it had huge serrated teeth that could slice through flesh with ease.

Carcharodontosaurus was named after the Greek word for the equally toothy Great White Shark.

Great white shark

It is thought Carcharodontosaurus needed at least 60kg of meat a day – the equivalent of about 50 roast chickens!

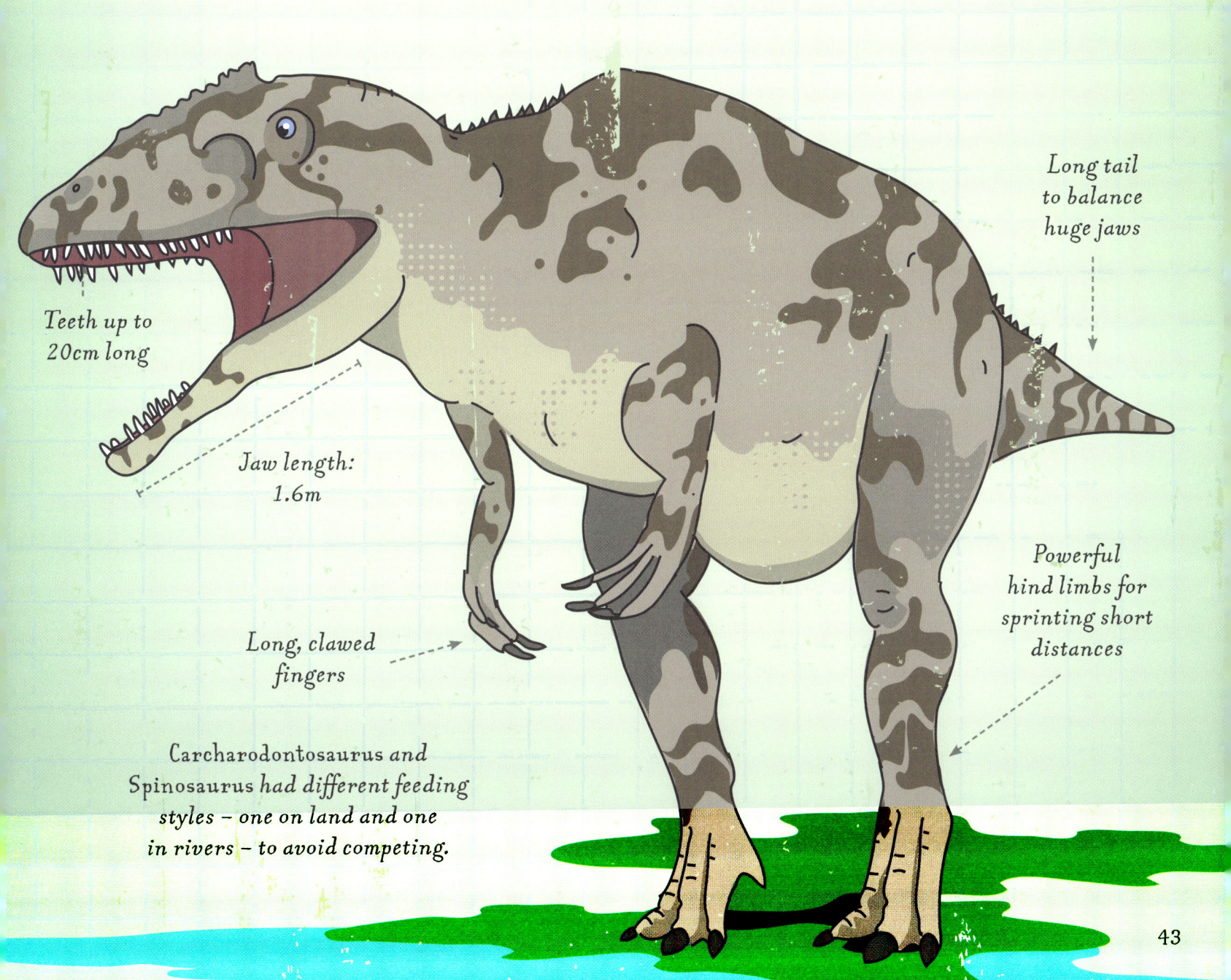

Long tail to balance huge jaws

Teeth up to 20cm long

Jaw length: 1.6m

Long, clawed fingers

Powerful hind limbs for sprinting short distances

Carcharodontosaurus and Spinosaurus had different feeding styles – one on land and one in rivers – to avoid competing.

43

Majungasaurus crenatissimus

Group: Theropod • Period: Cretaceous
Pronunciation: Mah-jung-ah-sore-us cren-at-is-see-mus

Majungasaurus had tiny arms, but its huge, formidable jaws more than made up for them. Bite marks reveal it may even have preyed on its own kind, providing one of the rare examples of dinosaur cannibalism! Unlike other theropods, *Majungasaurus* had a single horn on its head, probably used to impress a mate.

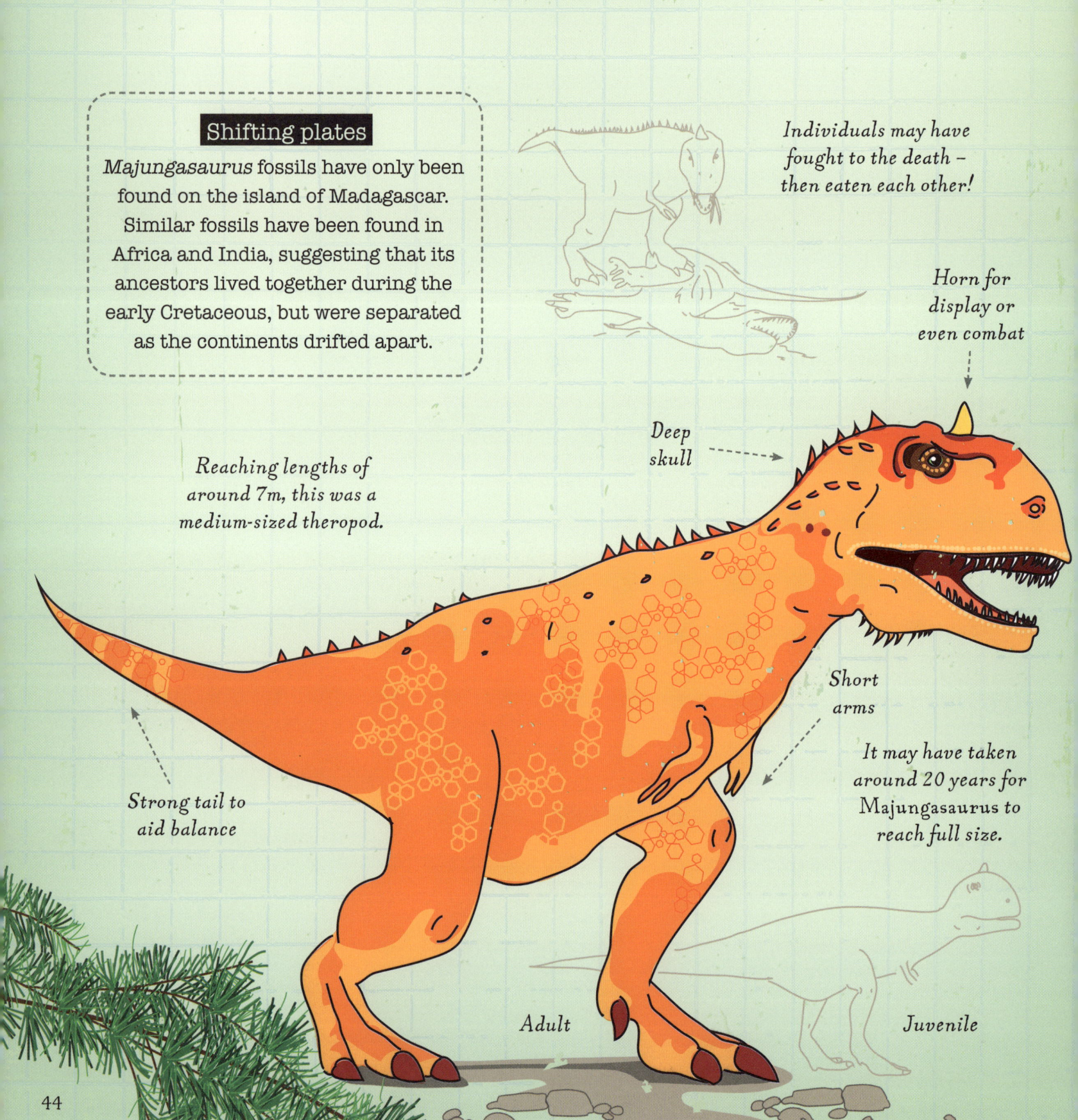

Shifting plates

Majungasaurus fossils have only been found on the island of Madagascar. Similar fossils have been found in Africa and India, suggesting that its ancestors lived together during the early Cretaceous, but were separated as the continents drifted apart.

Individuals may have fought to the death – then eaten each other!

Horn for display or even combat

Deep skull

Reaching lengths of around 7m, this was a medium-sized theropod.

Short arms

It may have taken around 20 years for Majungasaurus to reach full size.

Strong tail to aid balance

Adult

Juvenile

44

Massospondylus carinatus

Group: Sauropod • Period: Jurassic
Pronunciation: Mass-oh-spon-die-lus car-ee-nay-tus

Unlike later sauropods, with their huge bodies and thick legs, *Massospondylus* walked on just its hind limbs and had a fairly narrow body. It had a small, sharp claw on each of its forefeet, which it might have used for defence or for scraping food off plants. It had a fairly long neck, and probably used its tail as a counter-weight when reaching up to feed.

Trend-setter
Massospondylus was named by famous dinosaur discoverer Sir Richard Owen in 1854. It was one of the first dinosaurs ever to be classified.

Massospondylus is a well-studied dinosaur, with over 80 fossils found worldwide.

Bipedal stance

Small head

Long neck to reach food high in the trees

At 5m long, Massospondylus was small for a sauropod.

Embryo inside egg

Eggs found in 1976 contain the oldest dinosaur embryos ever found.

45

Paralititan stromeri

Group: Sauropod • Period: Cretaceous
Pronunciation: Pah-ral-i-tie-tan stro-mer-eye

Like many sauropods, *Paralititan* competes for the status of one of the largest animals ever. The remains of this dinosaur were discovered in part of an ancient mangrove swamp in Egypt, leading to its name, which means 'tidal giant'. Its skeleton showed evidence that *Paralititan* was scavenged or preyed upon by predators such as *Spinosaurus*.

Its shin bone was 1.69m long – as tall as an adult human.

26m

Paralititan was nearly as long as 8 African elephants.

Paralititan is the only dinosaur we know of that lived in a mangrove swamp.

Broad, barrel-shaped body

Small head with wide mouth for raking in foliage

It would have eaten almost non-stop to sustain its size.

Lesothosaurus diagnosticus

Group: Ornithischian • Period: Jurassic
Pronunciation: Less-oo-too-sore-us die-ag-noh-stik-us

The herbivore *Lesothosaurus* was one of the earliest, most primitive species of ornithischian. It was a small, bipedal dinosaur, far removed from the huge quadrupedal ornithischians of later years. Grazing on ferns, and using its speed to run from predators, it probably lived much like modern deer.

The name Lesothosaurus means the 'lizard from Lesotho', after the Kingdom of Lesotho where it was first discovered.

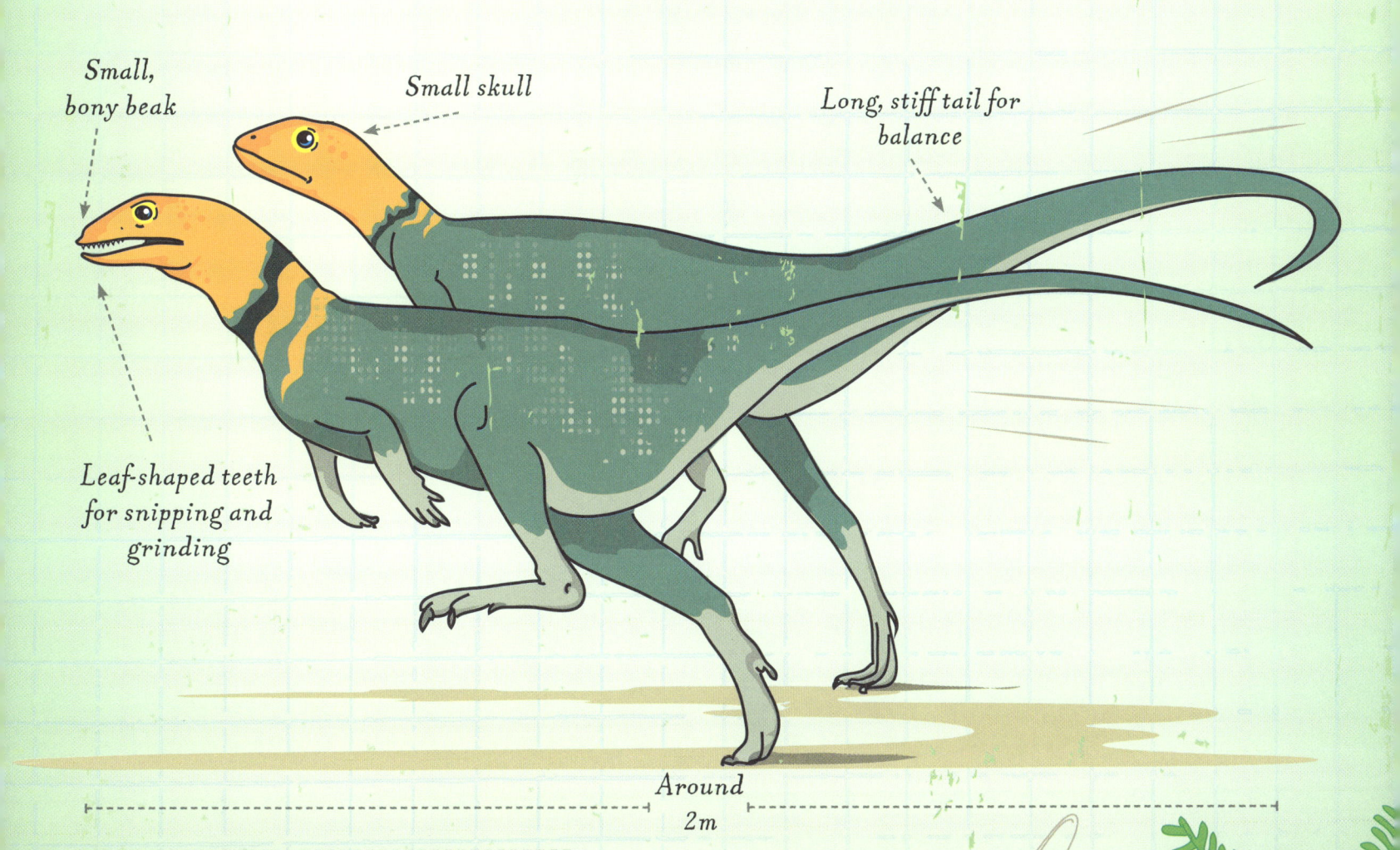

Small, bony beak

Small skull

Long, stiff tail for balance

Leaf-shaped teeth for snipping and grinding

Around 2m

Out for the count
The fossil remains of two *Lesothosaurus* were found curled up together in a cave. It is thought they may have been hibernating during the hottest months of the year.

It probably ate plants like grass and ferns, and sometimes insects.

Ouranosaurus nigeriensis

Group: Ornithischian • Period: Cretaceous
Pronunciation: Oo-ran-oh-sore-us nie-jeer-ee-en-sis

Ouranosaurus was a large herbivore, easily identified by the sail running down its back. This was supported by long spines on the top of each vertebra (back bone). *Ouranosaurus* grew to around 8 metres in length, and might have been the prey of choice for large predators such as *Carcharodontosaurus*.

In the family

Ouranosaurus was related to European and North American species such as *Iguanodon*. Like other iguanodonts, it could run on two or four legs.

Ouranosaurus's skeleton shows its extended vertebrae.

Sail height: up to 63cm

Beak with teeth at back for grinding tough plants

Its sail may have helped it cool down or warm up, or could have been used for display.

Tiny thumb spikes

Around 7m

Kentrosaurus aethiopicus

Group: Ornithischian • Period: Jurassic
Pronunciation: Ken-troh-sore-us ay-thee-ow-pik-us

Like its cousin *Stegosaurus*, *Kentrosaurus* had an array of bony plates along its spine. It also had huge spikes sticking out from its shoulders, and tail spikes called thagomizers which it could have swung at any dinosaur that dared to get too close. These defences, plus its 4.5-metre-long bulk, meant it could defend itself against all but the largest predators.

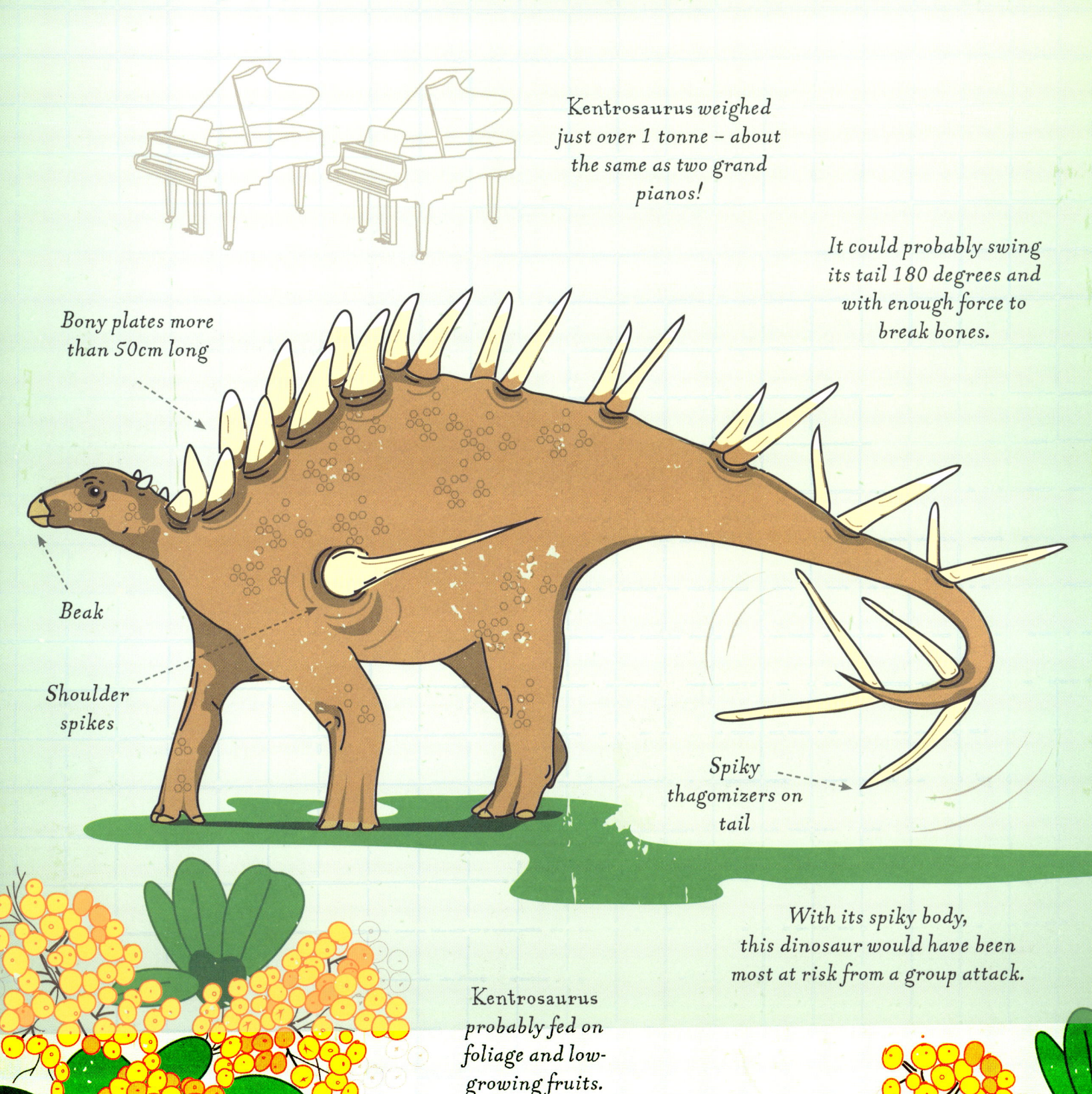

Kentrosaurus weighed just over 1 tonne – about the same as two grand pianos!

It could probably swing its tail 180 degrees and with enough force to break bones.

Bony plates more than 50cm long

Beak

Shoulder spikes

Spiky thagomizers on tail

With its spiky body, this dinosaur would have been most at risk from a group attack.

Kentrosaurus probably fed on foliage and low-growing fruits.

Phosphatodraco mauritanicus

Group: Pterosaur • Period: Cretaceous
Pronunciation: Phoss-phayt-oh-dray-ko more-it-an-ik-us

The first ever fossils of this giant pterosaur were discovered in Morocco, buried in huge deposits of the mineral phosphate. This is why its name means 'phosphate dragon'. It had a wingspan of around 5 metres, and a huge, pointed beak for snapping up prey – just like modern birds such as pelicans have today.

Around 5m

Many pterosaurs had elaborate crests, which helped to attract mates.

Phosphatodraco's large wings enabled it to glide effortlessly on warm air currents.

Long neck

Large pointed beak

It could walk on all fours as well as fly.

Heron

Phosphatodraco's long neck may have let it swing its head without moving its body. This is how herons hunt today.

Preserved footprints help scientists to see how Phosphatodraco walked, and the pose it used when taking off.

Alcione elainus

Group: Pterosaur • Period: Cretaceous
Pronunciation: Al-see-ow-ne e-line-us

Alcione was a smaller pterosaur that lived alongside giants such as *Phosphatodraco* in the skies over what is now Morocco. Together these species provide new evidence that pterosaurs were thriving across North Africa until the end of the Cretaceous Period.

Alcione

Golden eagle

With a wingspan of about 2m, *Alcione* was about the same size as a golden eagle.

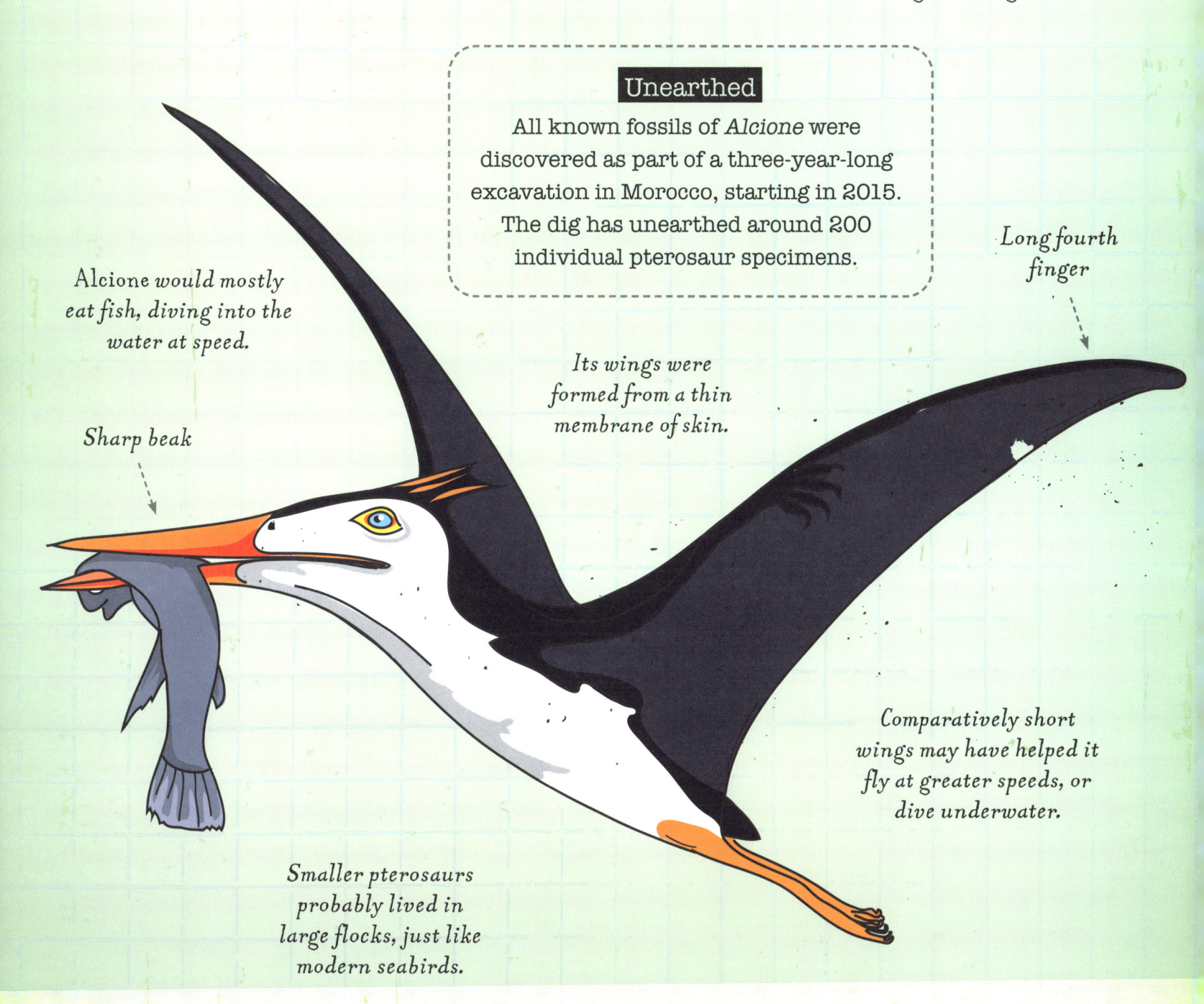

Unearthed
All known fossils of *Alcione* were discovered as part of a three-year-long excavation in Morocco, starting in 2015. The dig has unearthed around 200 individual pterosaur specimens.

Alcione would mostly eat fish, diving into the water at speed.

Sharp beak

Its wings were formed from a thin membrane of skin.

Long fourth finger

Comparatively short wings may have helped it fly at greater speeds, or dive underwater.

Smaller pterosaurs probably lived in large flocks, just like modern seabirds.

Angolasaurus bocagei

Group: Mosasaur • Period: Cretaceous
Pronunciation: An-gow-law-sore-us boh-cagg-ee-i

This mosasaur was one of the few species with a wide geographic range. It would have swum around the early Atlantic Ocean, which formed as South America and Africa began to pull away from each other millions of years ago. *Angolasaurus* was relatively small, at only 4 metres long, but was still a ferocious predator.

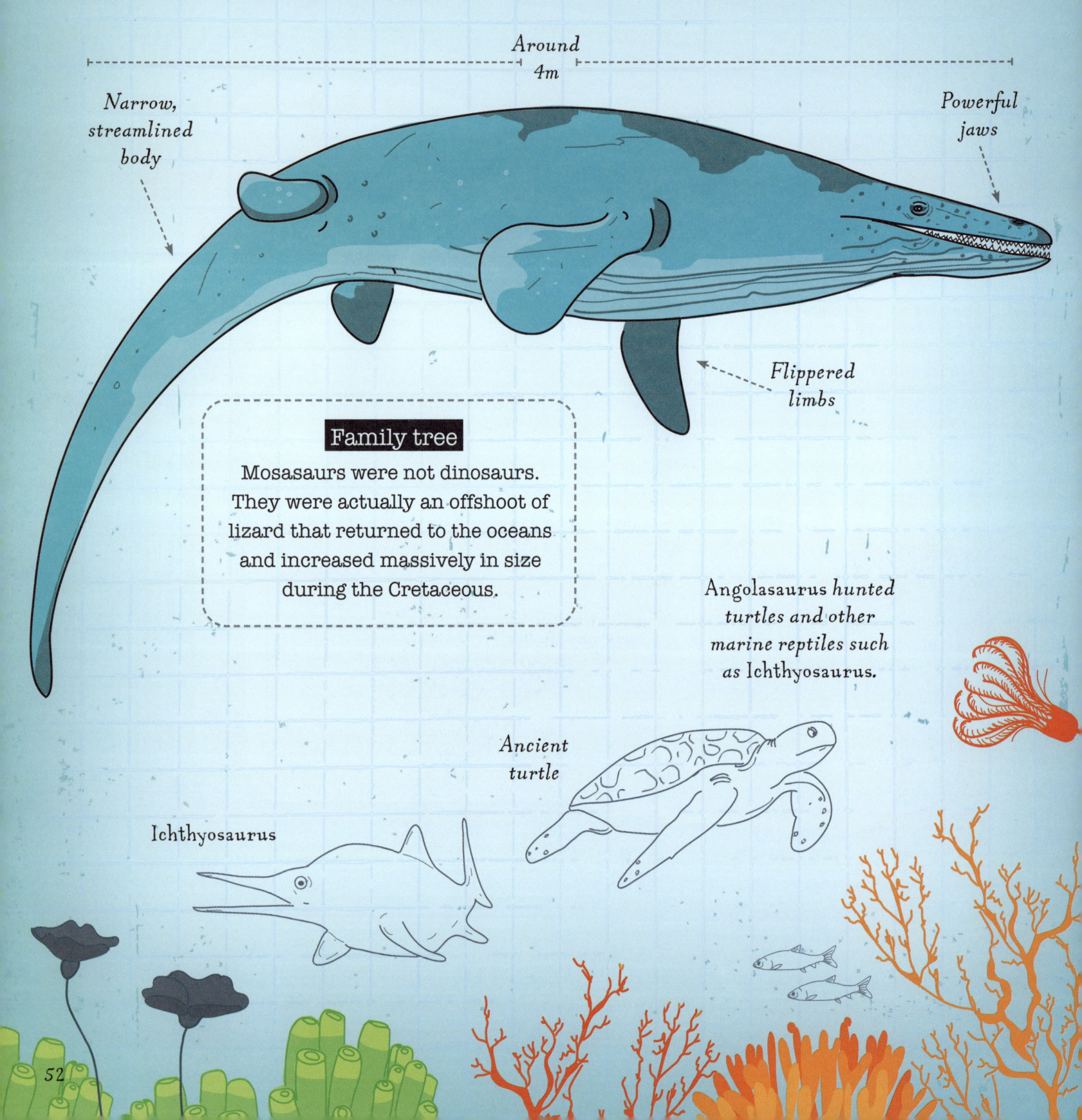

Around 4m

Narrow, streamlined body

Powerful jaws

Flippered limbs

Family tree

Mosasaurs were not dinosaurs. They were actually an offshoot of lizard that returned to the oceans and increased massively in size during the Cretaceous.

Angolasaurus hunted turtles and other marine reptiles such as Ichthyosaurus.

Ichthyosaurus

Ancient turtle

Sarcosuchus imperator

Group: Crocodyliform • Period: Cretaceous
Pronunciation: Sar-koh-sook-us im-per-at-ore

An ancestor of modern crocodiles, *Sarcosuchus* was one of the largest species of its kind ever to exist. It was twice as long as a modern saltwater crocodile, reaching lengths of up to 12 metres, and weighing around 8 tonnes. This ambush predator lived in lush, tropical rainforest in what is now the Sahara Desert.

It is likely that Sarcosuchus would have fought the huge dinosaurs it lived alongside.

Its bite force was probably stronger than that of most meat-eating dinosaurs.

Huge skull with more than 100 teeth

Armour plating along its back for protection

Around 12m

Despite its size, it could probably hide nine-tenths of its body underwater.

Saltwater crocodile

6m

ATLANTIC OCEAN

Asia

Europe, North America and Asia together made up the northern supercontinent know as Laurasia. But during the Jurassic Period, much of what we call Asia simply did not exist – it was either underwater or hadn't yet formed. Throughout the Cretaceous, Asia was separated from the southern supercontinent Gondwana by the Tethys Ocean, and had unique and wonderful dinosaur fauna. Many dinosaurs from Asia have now been found with the fossilised remains of feathers, which may have evolved to help adapt to cooler climates at the time.

Key

1. Azhdarcho lancicollis
2. Sinosauropteryx prima
3. Halszkaraptor escuilliei
4. Haubeisaurus allocotus
5. Therizinosaurus cheloniformis
6. Shastasaurus liangae

Sinosauropteryx prima

Group: Theropod • Period: Cretaceous
Pronunciation: Sigh-no-sore-op-ter-iks pree-mah

Sinosauropteryx was one of the first dinosaurs to be discovered with evidence of hair-like bristles similar to feathers – just like the kind you would find on a baby chicken. Incredibly we even know what colour these bristles were, enabling us to piece together a good picture of this small hunter.

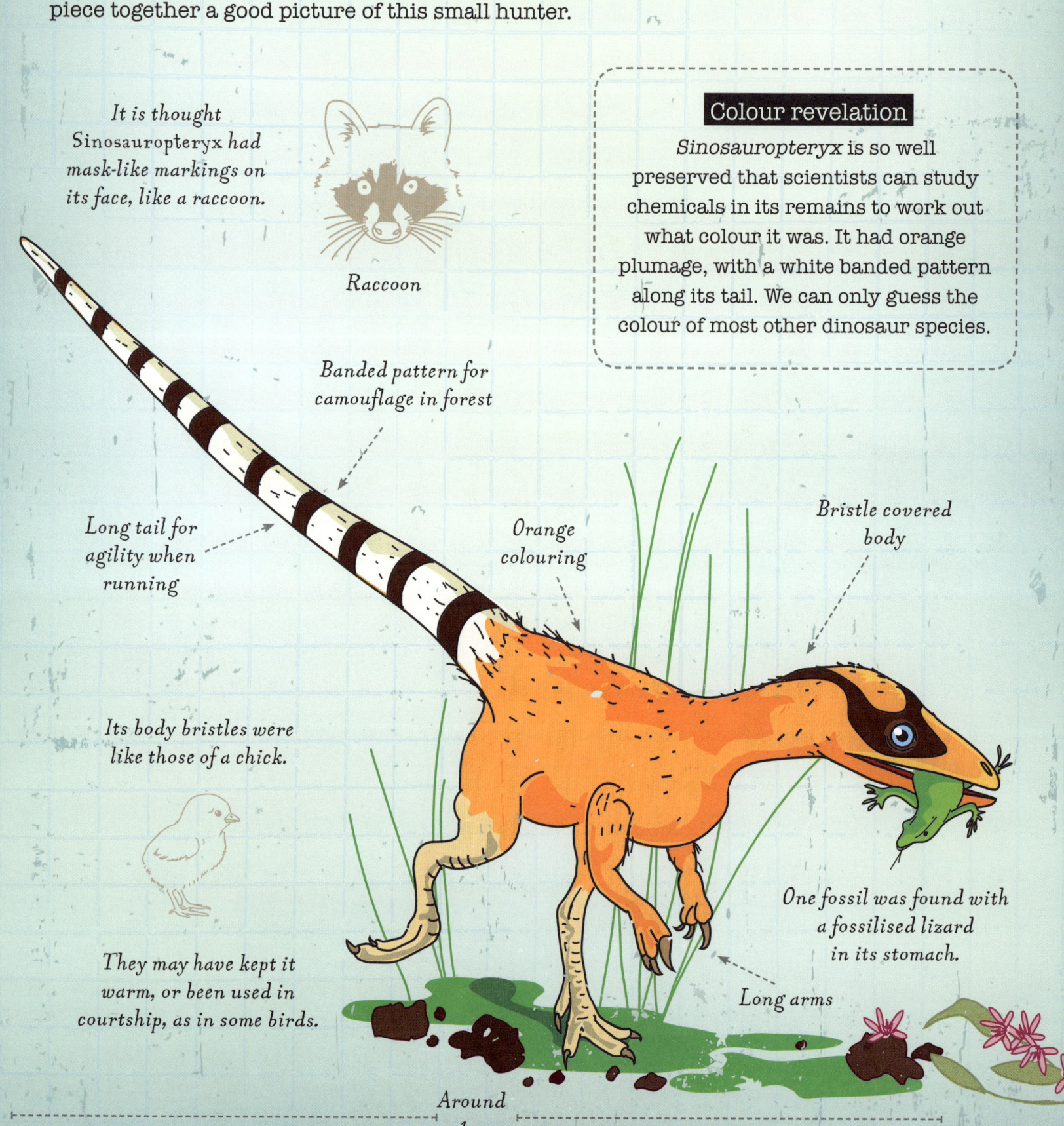

It is thought Sinosauropteryx had mask-like markings on its face, like a raccoon.

Raccoon

Colour revelation

Sinosauropteryx is so well preserved that scientists can study chemicals in its remains to work out what colour it was. It had orange plumage, with a white banded pattern along its tail. We can only guess the colour of most other dinosaur species.

Banded pattern for camouflage in forest

Long tail for agility when running

Orange colouring

Bristle covered body

Its body bristles were like those of a chick.

One fossil was found with a fossilised lizard in its stomach.

Long arms

They may have kept it warm, or been used in courtship, as in some birds.

Around 1m

56

Therizinosaurus cheloniformis

Group: Theropod • Period: Cretaceous
Pronunciation: Thair-uh-zeen-uh-sore-us chel-oh-nee-fore-miss

At first glance *Therizinosaurus* looks like the ultimate killing machine, with the huge scythe-like claws on its forelimbs. But these were probably for raking in foliage, or fighting off danger, rather than attacking prey. In fact, unlike most other theropods, *Therizinosaurus* probably ate more plants than meat!

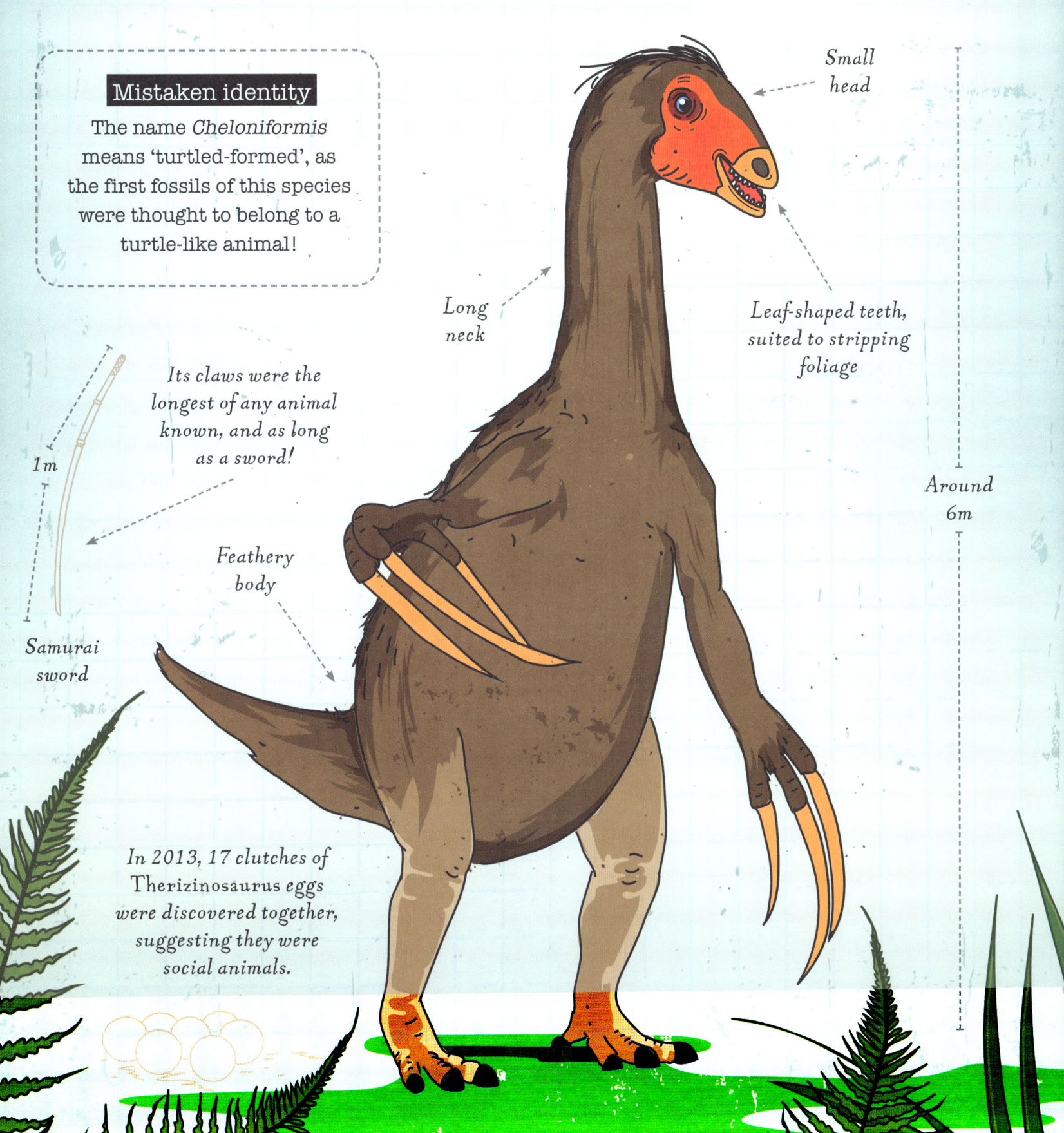

Mistaken identity

The name *Cheloniformis* means 'turtled-formed', as the first fossils of this species were thought to belong to a turtle-like animal!

Its claws were the longest of any animal known, and as long as a sword!

1m

Samurai sword

Feathery body

Small head

Long neck

Leaf-shaped teeth, suited to stripping foliage

Around 6m

In 2013, 17 clutches of *Therizinosaurus* eggs were discovered together, suggesting they were social animals.

Velociraptor mongoliensis

Group: Theropod • Period: Cretaceous
Pronunciation: Veh-loss-ee-rap-tor mon-goh-lee-en-siss

Fast, agile and deadly, *Velociraptor* was a well-honed predator from the ancient deserts of Mongolia. It had a feathery body and its feet were equipped with long sickle-shaped claws, which it used to pin down its prey and disembowel them.

One specimen's fossil was found in a death embrace with a Protoceratops. They were probably buried in a landslide as they fought.

Protoceratops

Velociraptor

Long, narrow skull

Long tail for balance

Feathery body and winglike arms

It held its killing claw up when it walked, to avoid blunting it.

Killing claw

Actual size killing claw (6cm)

Dead famous

Velociraptor was made famous by the film *Jurassic Park* where it was depicted as large and scaly. In fact, it was only the size of a turkey and covered in feathers!

Caihong juji

Group: Theropod • Period: Jurassic
Pronunciation: Khi-hong joo-jee

The name '*Caihong*' is Mandarin for 'rainbow', and refers to the incredible colours found in fossils of this dinosaur's feathers. It was a small dinosaur, no more than half a metre long and resembling a cross between a hummingbird and a crow. It might have been one of the earliest dinosaurs capable of gliding from tree to tree.

Caihong had iridescent feathers like a hummingbird.

Ruby-throated hummingbird

Bony crests, possibly for displaying to mates

Long, feathery tail

Feathered wings

Caihong could probably glide between trees, much like a flying squirrel today.

Its fossils were discovered surrounded by intact feathers. Before this, scientists had only found feather impressions.

Flying squirrel

59

Halszkaraptor escuilliei

Group: Theropod • Period: Cretaceous
Pronunciation: Haltz-kah-rap-tor ess-kwee-lee-ee-eye

At first glance, *Halszkaraptor* looks like a modern goose, with its small body, long neck, feathers and beak. However, it was more closely related to *Velociraptor* than to modern birds. It had a semi-aquatic lifestyle and was able to paddle with its flippered forelimbs, though it probably spent most of its time waddling on land.

Small sharp teeth would have helped it grab tiny fish.

Beak

Halszkaraptor probably fed on fish, crustaceans, small mammals and reptiles.

Short wing-like forelimbs like a penguin's

Long swan-like neck

Feathery tail

Strong hindlimbs

It could have floated on water and was about the size of a modern duck.

Mallard duck

Huabeisaurus allocotus

Group: Sauropod • **Period:** Cretaceous
Pronunciation: Hwa-bay-sore-us al-oh-coh-tus

At 20 metres in length, *Huabeisaurus* was a true giant from Cretaceous China. It is one of the most complete Asian sauropods known, which makes it an important find. Making up nearly half of its body length, its neck was perfectly adapted for reaching leaves high in the treetops.

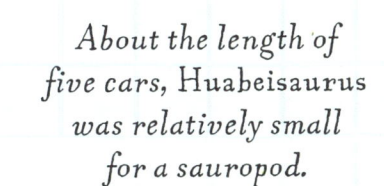

About the length of five cars, Huabeisaurus was relatively small for a sauropod.

20m

Small head with large jaws

Long neck

Bulky, barrel-shaped body

What's in a name?
Huabeisaurus was discovered in the province of Shanxi in northeastern China. Its name means 'Northern Chinese Lizard'.

It walked on four legs to support its weight.

CHINA

Mamenchisaurus constructus

Group: Sauropod • Period: Jurassic
Pronunciation: Mah-men-chih-sore-us con-struck-tuss

Mamenchisaurus was one of the biggest sauropods known from the Jurassic period, growing up to 35 metres long and weighing up to 75 tonnes. The species name, *constructus*, refers to the fact that it was originally discovered during work on a highway construction site! At least six different species of *Mamenchisaurus* are known in varying sizes but also with enormously long necks.

Dino or dragon?

People have been discovering dinosaur fossils for hundreds of years – long before we knew what dinosaurs were. Across Asia, these fossils were often thought to be dragon bones!

Its neck bones were very light – in places they were as thin as eggshells!

Small head

Very long neck

Rounded body

Half of Mamenchisaurus's length was made up of its neck. This may have helped it reach plants across boggy land.

Long tree-trunk like legs

Huayangosaurus taibaii

Group: Ornithopod • Period: Jurassic
Pronunciation: Hwah-yang-oh-sore-us tie-bye-ee

A close relative of *Stegosaurus*, *Huayangosaurus* lived around 20 million years before its cousin, as well as on a completely different continent! It was smaller than Stegosaurus, but had a similar row of plates down its back. It also had a dangerously spiked tail for defence against predators.

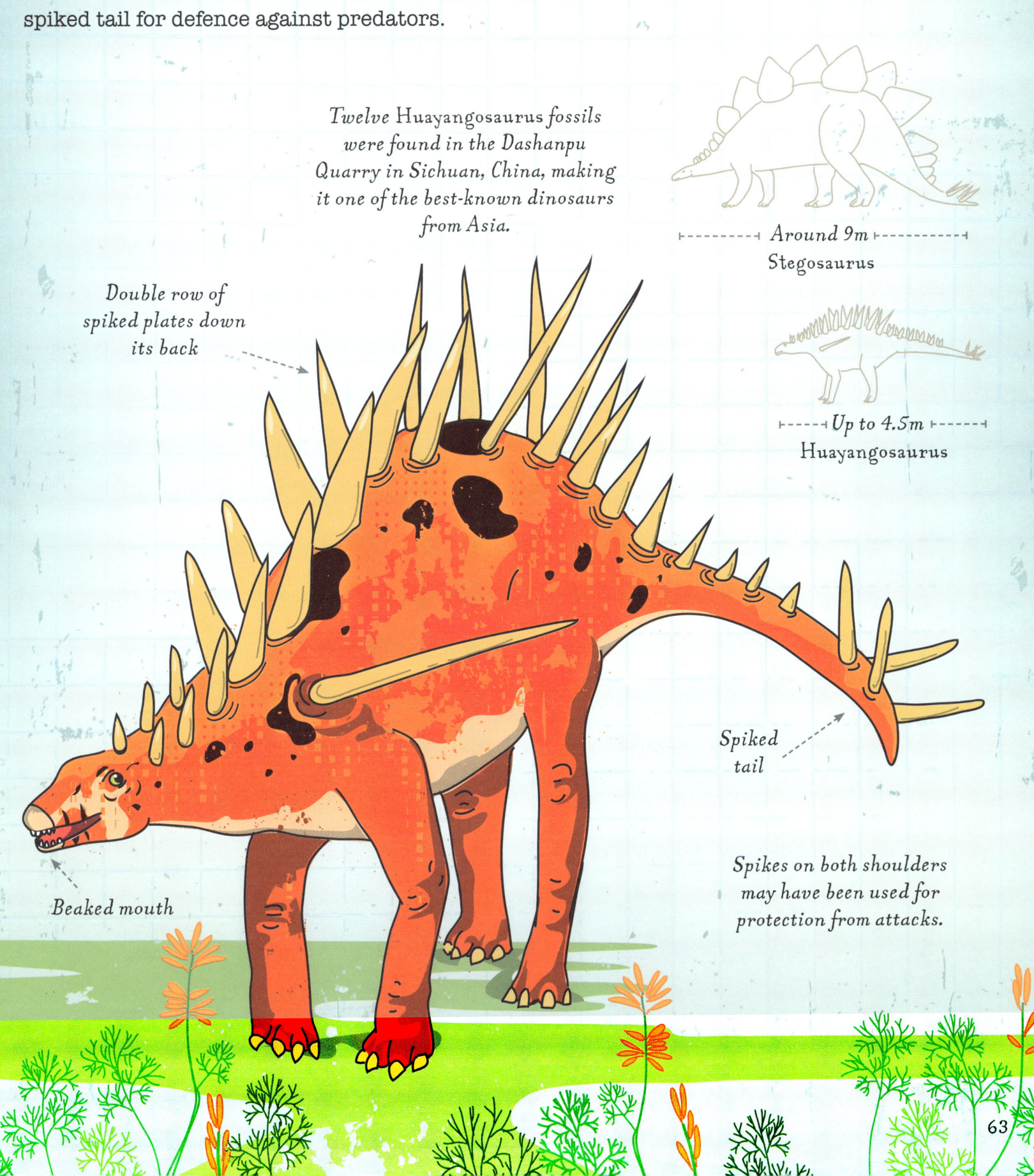

Twelve Huayangosaurus fossils were found in the Dashanpu Quarry in Sichuan, China, making it one of the best-known dinosaurs from Asia.

Around 9m
Stegosaurus

Up to 4.5m
Huayangosaurus

Double row of spiked plates down its back

Spiked tail

Beaked mouth

Spikes on both shoulders may have been used for protection from attacks.

63

Protoceratops andrewsi

Group: Ornithischian • Period: Cretaceous
Pronunciation: Pro-toe-sair-uh-tops an-droo-siy

Unlike other ceratopsians, including its cousin *Triceratops*, *Protoceratops* lacked any big horns on its face, though it did have a protective head frill. The discovery of large numbers of *Protoceratops* skeletons together suggests these dinosaurs would have moved in herds through the deserts of ancient Mongolia, just like many herbivores today.

Bristly tail

Large frill for defence against predators, and possibly for attracting mates.

Beak for slicing tough leaves

Juvenile Protoceratops

Adults grew to around 1.8m long – about the size of a sheep.

A nest of 15 young Protoceratops suggests these dinosaurs cared for their young.

Psittacosaurus mongoliensis

Group: Ornithischian • Period: Cretaceous
Pronunciation: Sit-ah-koh-sore-us mon-goh-lee-en-siss

Psittacosaurus was probably one of the earliest ancestors of ceratopsians like *Triceratops*. Its name translates as 'parrot lizard', in reference to its large beak. Almost uniquely among ornithischians, it had a tail covered in long, bristle-like structures, similar to those seen in animals like porcupines today.

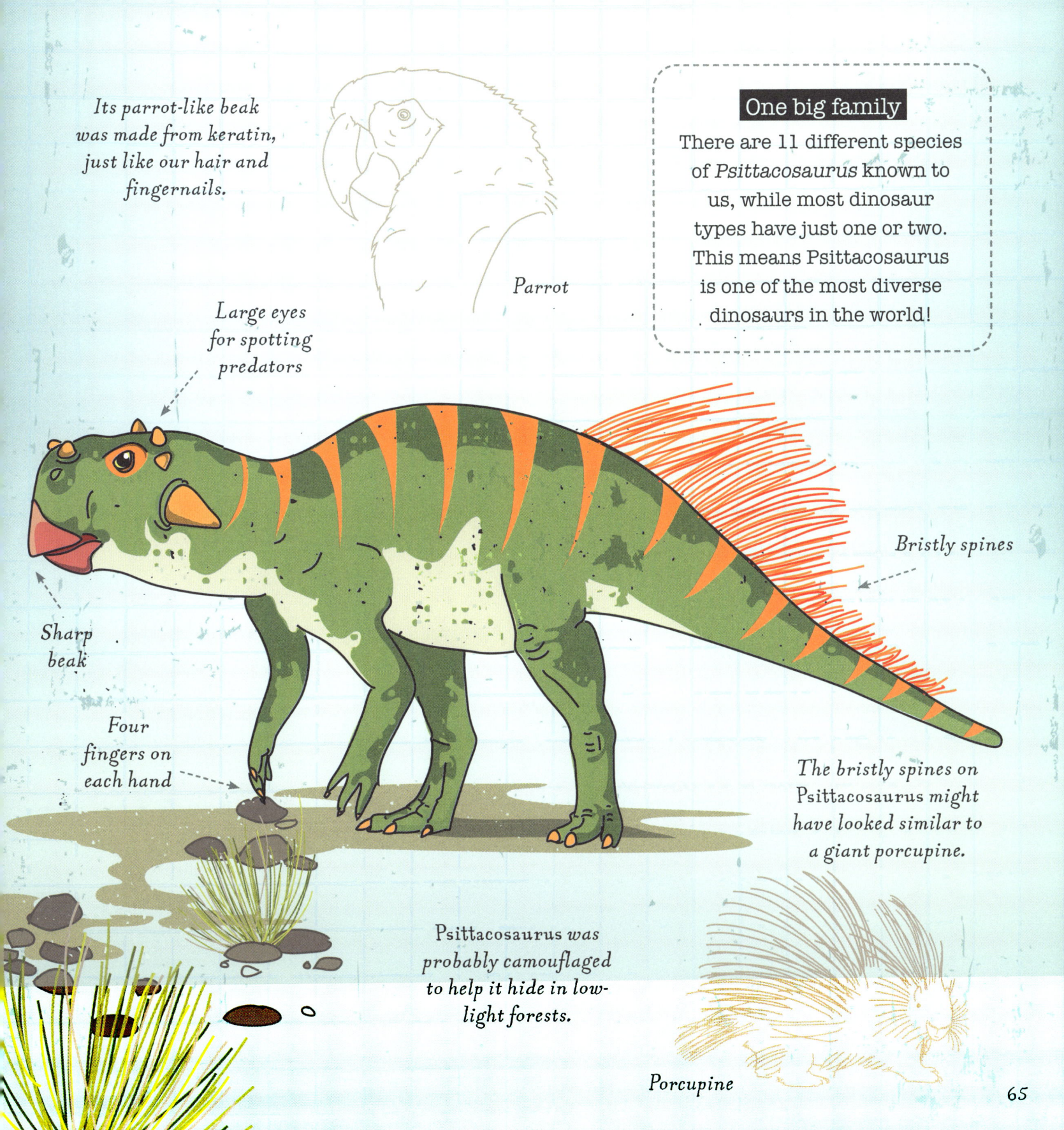

Its parrot-like beak was made from keratin, just like our hair and fingernails.

Parrot

One big family

There are 11 different species of *Psittacosaurus* known to us, while most dinosaur types have just one or two. This means Psittacosaurus is one of the most diverse dinosaurs in the world!

Large eyes for spotting predators

Bristly spines

Sharp beak

Four fingers on each hand

The bristly spines on Psittacosaurus might have looked similar to a giant porcupine.

Psittacosaurus was probably camouflaged to help it hide in low-light forests.

Porcupine

65

Kryptodrakon progenitor

Group: Pterosaur • Period: Jurassic
Pronunciation: Crip-toe-dray-con proh-jen-it-ore

The name *Kryptodrakon* literally means 'hidden dragon' and refers to the famous martial arts movie, *Crouching Tiger Hidden Dragon* (the film was even shot on location in the same desert where the fossils were found). This 'hidden dragon' is actually one of the oldest and most primitive pterosaurs ever discovered. It was relatively small in size, with a wingspan of just 1.5 metres.

Upland Buzzard

Kryptodrakon

Kryptodrakon had the same wingspan as a buzzard.

Fossils of this species were originally mistaken for those of a theropod dinosaur.

Head crest

Long beak

Lightly built body, with hollow bones

Dinosaur death pit

The remains of *Kryptodrakon* were found in the so-called 'dinosaur death pits' of the Shishugou Formation in northwest China. Many bones from the Jurassic period have been found there.

Guidraco venator

Group: Pterosaur • Period: Cretaceous
Pronunciation: Gwee-dray-coh veh-nah-tore

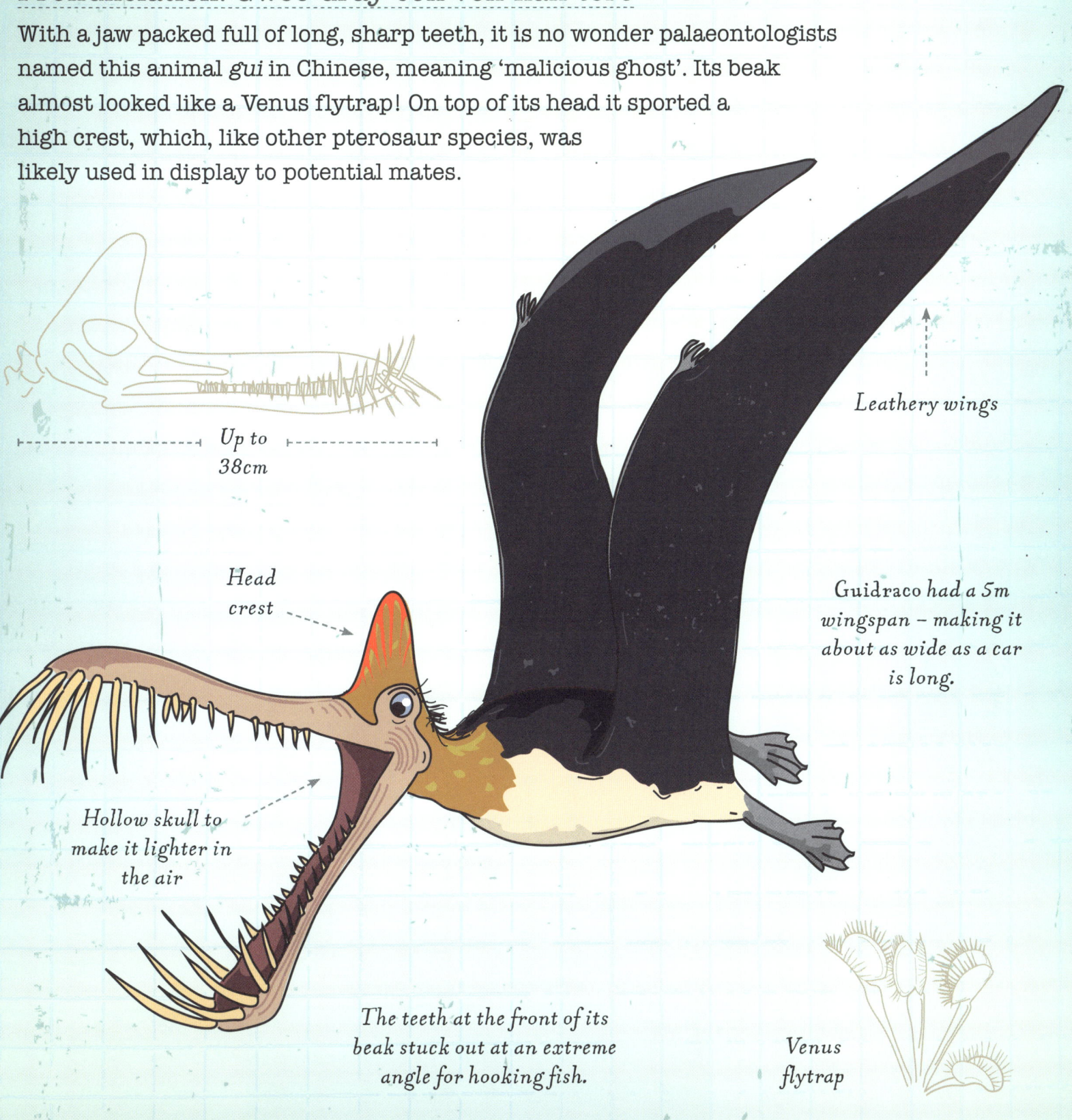

With a jaw packed full of long, sharp teeth, it is no wonder palaeontologists named this animal *gui* in Chinese, meaning 'malicious ghost'. Its beak almost looked like a Venus flytrap! On top of its head it sported a high crest, which, like other pterosaur species, was likely used in display to potential mates.

Up to 38cm

Head crest

Leathery wings

Guidraco had a 5m wingspan – making it about as wide as a car is long.

Hollow skull to make it lighter in the air

The teeth at the front of its beak stuck out at an extreme angle for hooking fish.

Venus flytrap

67

Azhdarcho lancicollis

Group: Pterosaur • Period: Cretaceous
Pronunciation: As-dar-ko lan-see-coh-liss

Azhdarcho can be identified by its uniquely elongated neck bones (vertebrae). In fact, *lancicollis* means 'spear neck' in Latin. Like other pterosaurs, the bones of *Azhdarcho* were nearly hollow, reducing its body weight so it could take to the air more easily.

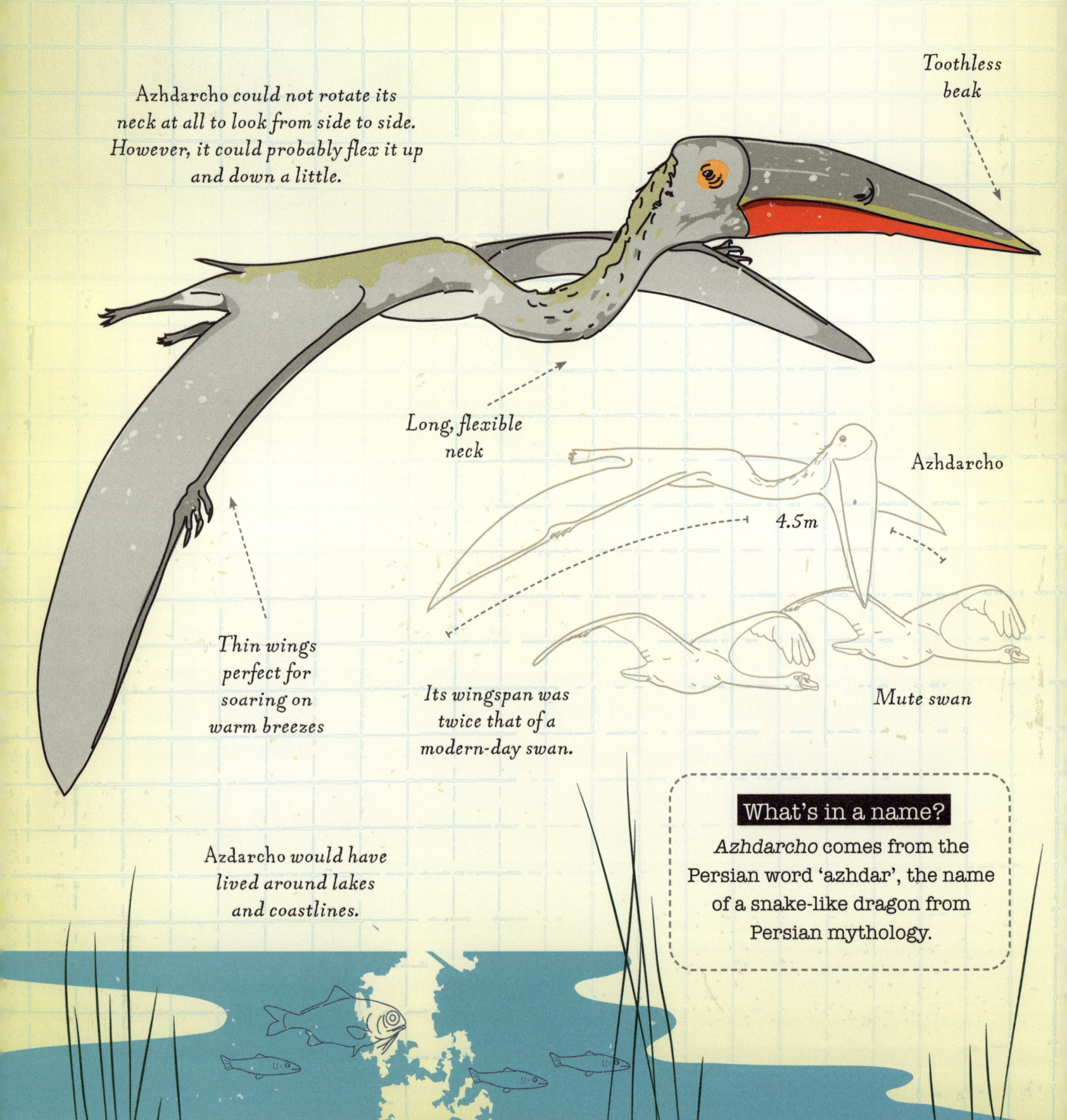

Azhdarcho could not rotate its neck at all to look from side to side. However, it could probably flex it up and down a little.

Toothless beak

Long, flexible neck

Thin wings perfect for soaring on warm breezes

Its wingspan was twice that of a modern-day swan.

Azhdarcho

4.5m

Mute swan

Azdarcho would have lived around lakes and coastlines.

What's in a name?

Azhdarcho comes from the Persian word 'azhdar', the name of a snake-like dragon from Persian mythology.

Shastasaurus liangae

Group: Ichthyosaur • Period: Triassic
Pronunciation: Sha-sta-sore-us lee-ang-aye

Shastasaurus was one of the largest marine reptiles of all time, with a maximum size estimated at 21 metres in length – almost as long as a blue whale! It had a short snout for catching fish, and flippers for helping it to manoeuvre its bulky body through the Triassic seas.

Today's blue whale is the largest animal that has ever lived on the Earth.

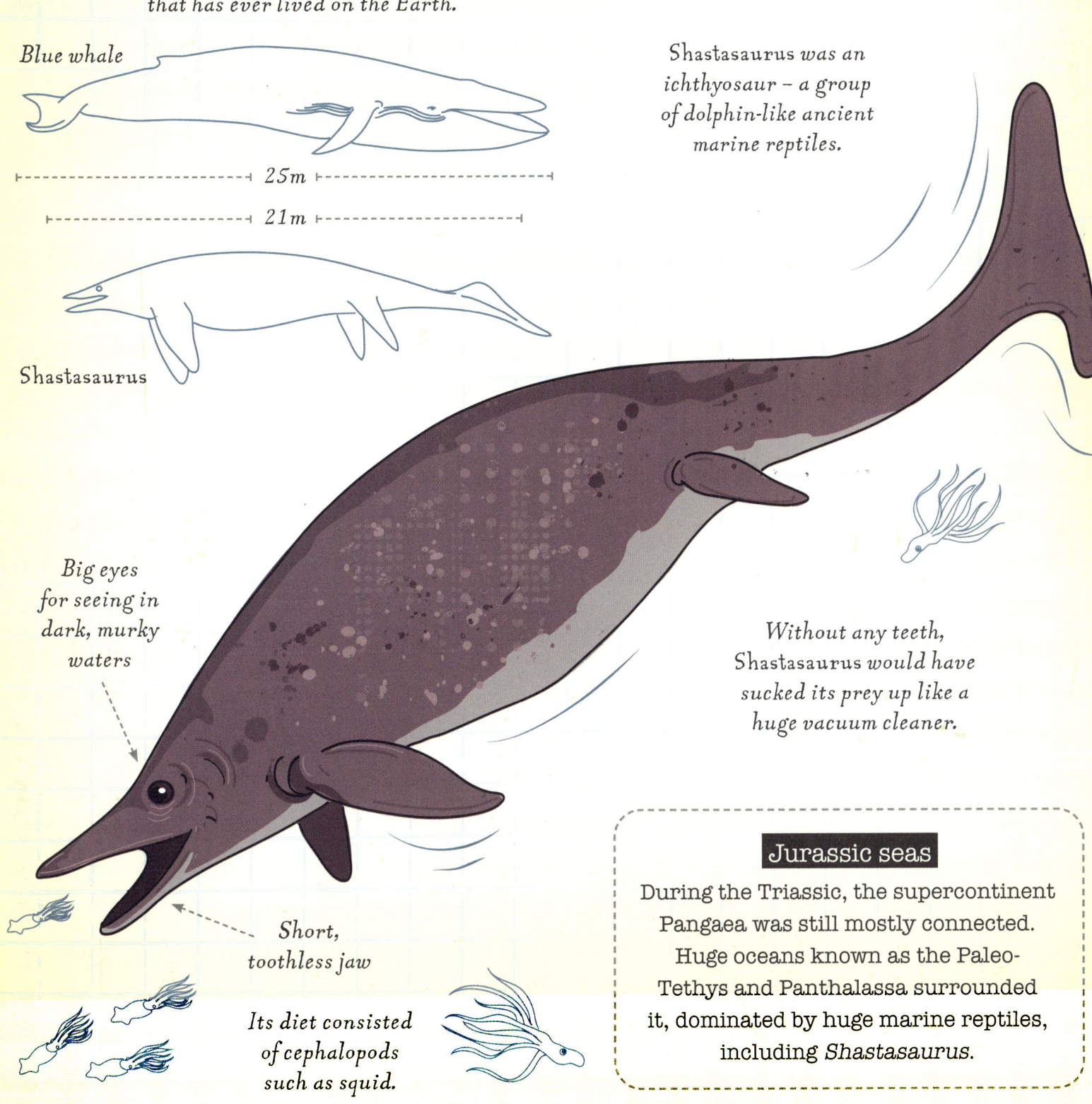

Blue whale
25m

21m
Shastasaurus

Shastasaurus was an ichthyosaur – a group of dolphin-like ancient marine reptiles.

Big eyes for seeing in dark, murky waters

Without any teeth, *Shastasaurus* would have sucked its prey up like a huge vacuum cleaner.

Short, toothless jaw

Its diet consisted of cephalopods such as squid.

Jurassic seas

During the Triassic, the supercontinent Pangaea was still mostly connected. Huge oceans known as the Paleo-Tethys and Panthalassa surrounded it, dominated by huge marine reptiles, including *Shastasaurus*.

Key

1. Balaur bondoc
2. Iguanodon bernissartensis
3. Hatzegopteryx thambema
4. Baryonyx walkeri
5. Compsognathus longipes
6. Archaeopteryx lithographica

ATLANTIC OCEAN

MEDITERRANEAN SEA

Europe

At the beginning of the Jurassic Period, Europe connected the large Asian and North American landmasses. However, as the climate changed and became warmer, sea levels rose, covering much of the land in warm, shallow seas. This meant that from the Middle Jurassic onwards, Europe existed as a cluster of islands covered in lush, green rainforests. Cut off from the rest of the globe, a huge variety of weird and wonderful dinosaurs evolved within this tropical paradise. Meanwhile, up in the skies, pterosaurs competed alongside the early ancestors of modern birds.

Baryonyx walkeri
Family: Theropod • Period: Cretaceous
Pronunciation: Ba-ri-on-iks wall-ker-eye

Baryonyx was the first ever fish-eating dinosaur to be discovered. It had long jaws like a crocodile with curved teeth for gripping slippery prey, and hooked claws for flicking fish from the water. Its snout was probably lined with sensory organs that would have helped it to detect movements in the water, similar to those seen in sharks today.

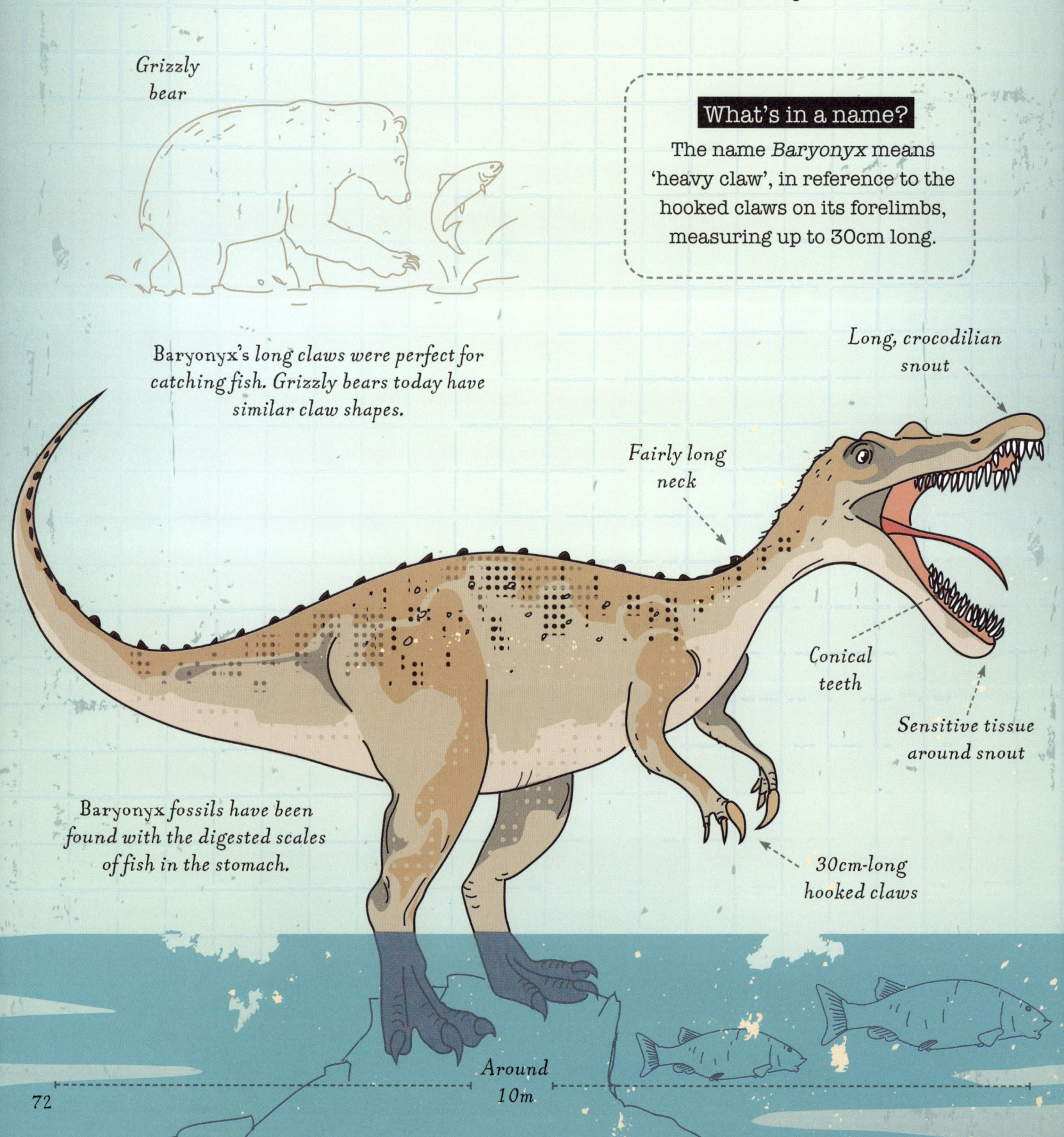

Grizzly bear

What's in a name?
The name *Baryonyx* means 'heavy claw', in reference to the hooked claws on its forelimbs, measuring up to 30cm long.

Baryonyx's long claws were perfect for catching fish. Grizzly bears today have similar claw shapes.

Long, crocodilian snout

Fairly long neck

Conical teeth

Sensitive tissue around snout

Baryonyx fossils have been found with the digested scales of fish in the stomach.

30cm-long hooked claws

Around 10m

Lilliensternus liliensterni

Family: Theropod • Period: Triassic
Pronunciation: Li-ly-en-stir-nus li-ly-en-stir-ny

One of the earliest known theropods and the largest meat-eater of its time, *Liliensternus* was a 5-metre-long predator with a serious appetite. In the Late Triassic period, there were still relatively few dinosaurs around, so *Liliensternus* probably tried its luck hunting large prey such as *Plateosaurus*, as well as smaller herbivores.

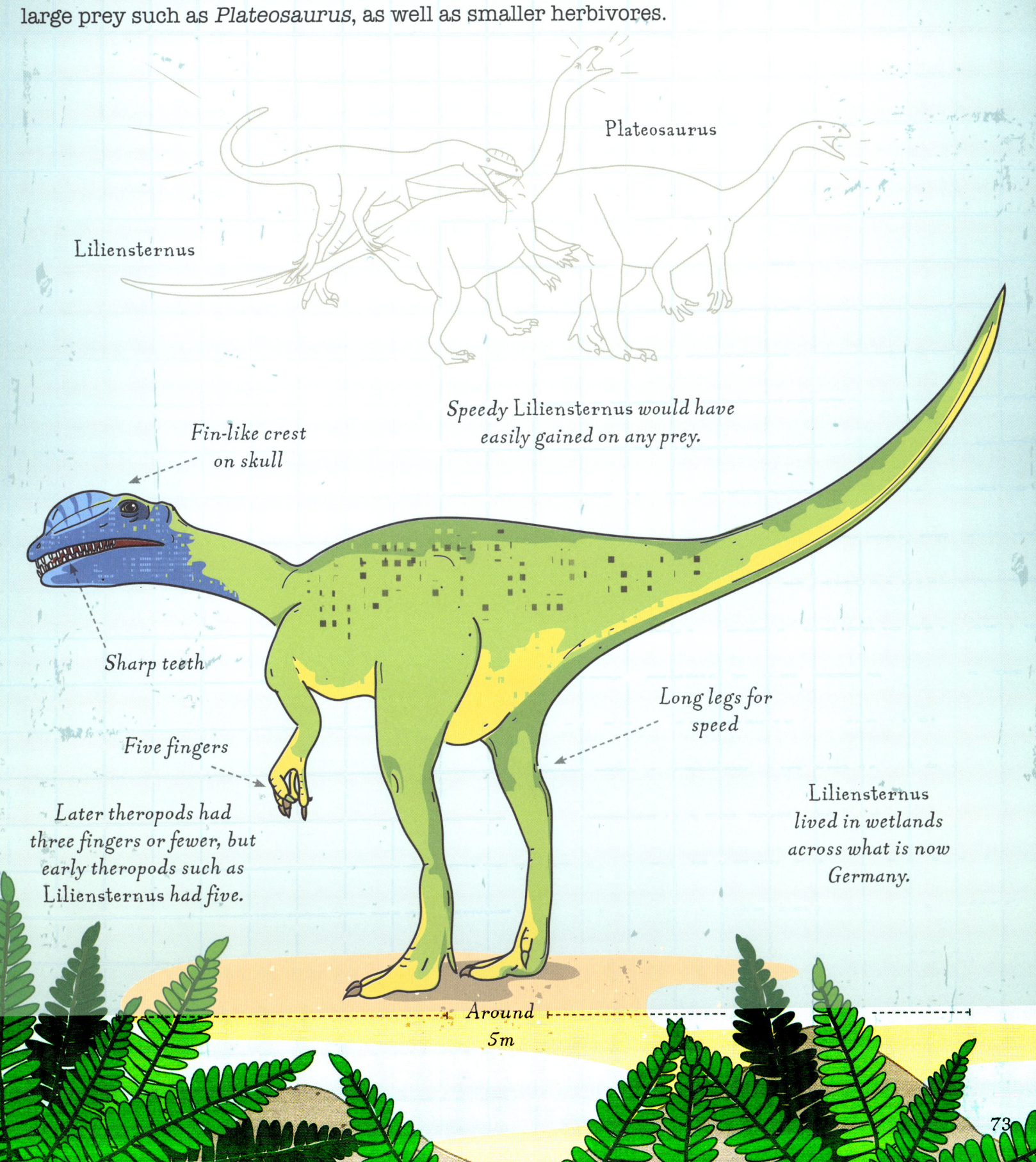

Liliensternus

Plateosaurus

Speedy Liliensternus would have easily gained on any prey.

Fin-like crest on skull

Sharp teeth

Long legs for speed

Five fingers

Later theropods had three fingers or fewer, but early theropods such as Liliensternus had five.

Liliensternus lived in wetlands across what is now Germany.

Around 5m

Compsognathus longipes

Family: Theropod • Period: Jurassic
Pronunciation: Comp-sug-nay-thus long-ee-pez

Compsognathus is a rare find for palaeontologists, with very few fossils discovered so far. At only 1 metre in length, it was the smallest known dinosaur until the 1990s. Judging by its close relatives, it is possible that *Compsognathus* had a body covered in fine, fur-like fibres, similar to the fur on mammals today.

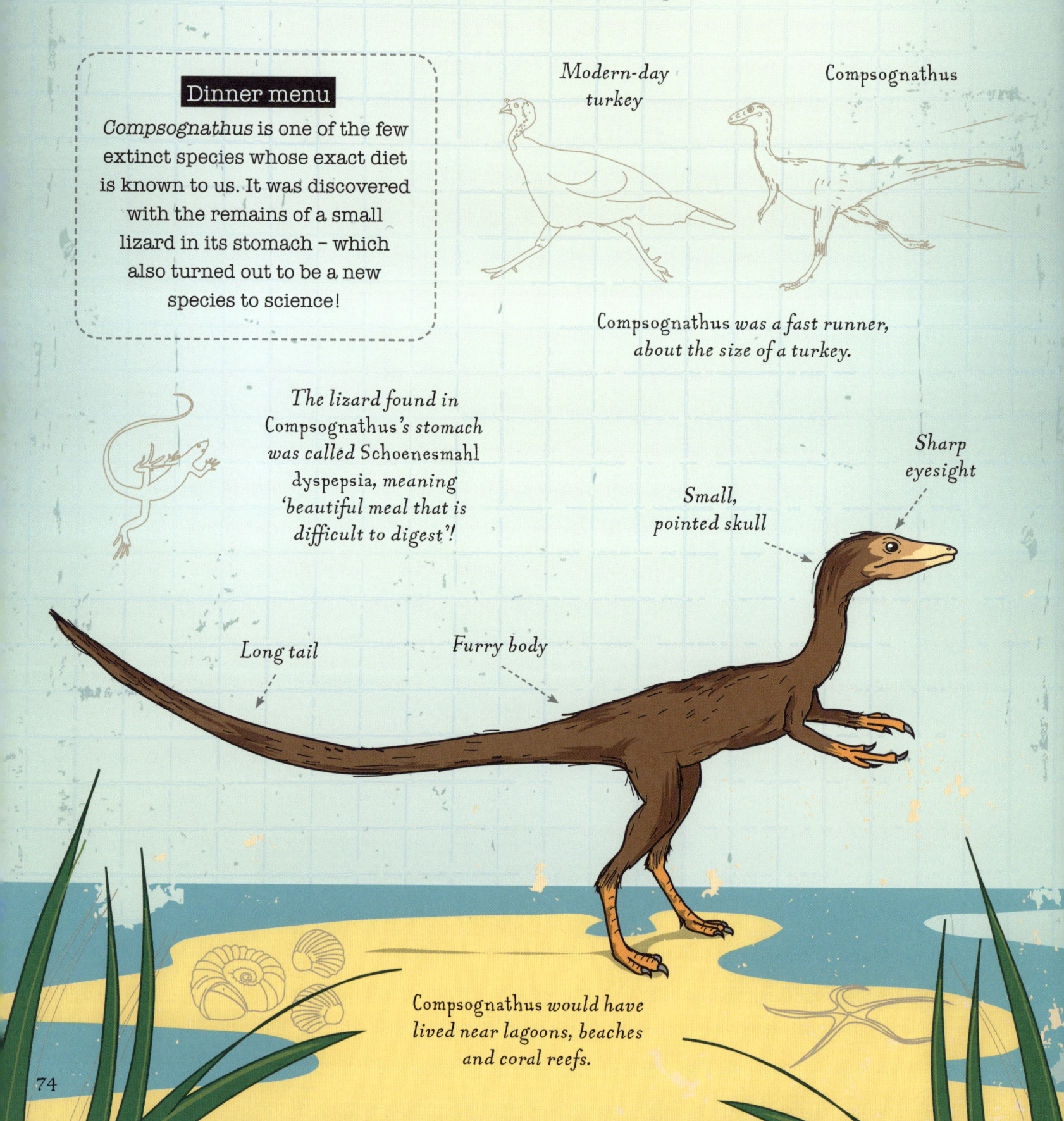

Dinner menu

Compsognathus is one of the few extinct species whose exact diet is known to us. It was discovered with the remains of a small lizard in its stomach – which also turned out to be a new species to science!

Modern-day turkey

Compsognathus

Compsognathus was a fast runner, about the size of a turkey.

The lizard found in Compsognathus's stomach was called *Schoenesmahl dyspepsia*, meaning 'beautiful meal that is difficult to digest'!

Sharp eyesight

Small, pointed skull

Long tail

Furry body

Compsognathus would have lived near lagoons, beaches and coral reefs.

74

Balaur bondoc

Family: Theropod • Period: Cretaceous
Pronunciation: Ba-la-ur bon-dok

Balaur is named after a dragon from Romanian folklore, and rightly so – with a wicked set of teeth, and double sickle-clawed feet, it was a predator sure to inspire terror. Compared to its cousins of a similar size, such as *Velociraptor*, *Balaur* was relatively chunky.

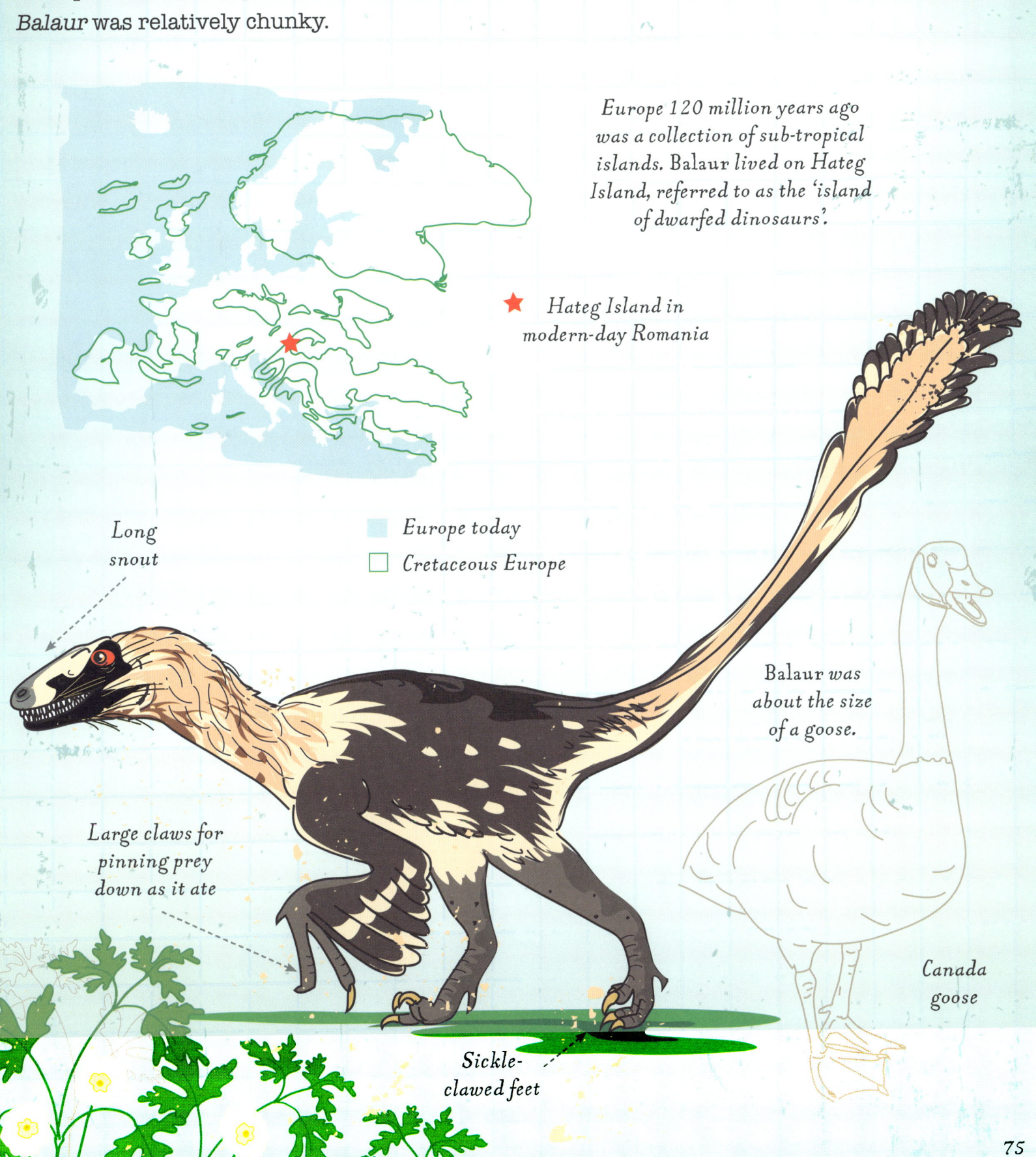

Europe 120 million years ago was a collection of sub-tropical islands. Balaur lived on Hateg Island, referred to as the 'island of dwarfed dinosaurs'.

★ Hateg Island in modern-day Romania

■ Europe today
□ Cretaceous Europe

Long snout

Large claws for pinning prey down as it ate

Sickle-clawed feet

Balaur was about the size of a goose.

Canada goose

75

Archaeopteryx lithographica

Family: Theropod • Period: Jurassic
Pronunciation: Ar-key-op-ter-iks lith-o-gra-phi-ka

Archaeopteryx is an incredible dinosaur specimen, often hailed as the 'missing link' between dinosaurs and birds. It had a long, bony tail, and teeth just like a dinosaur, but also had a beak and feathers like a bird. Scientists are still not certain whether it could have flown or not.

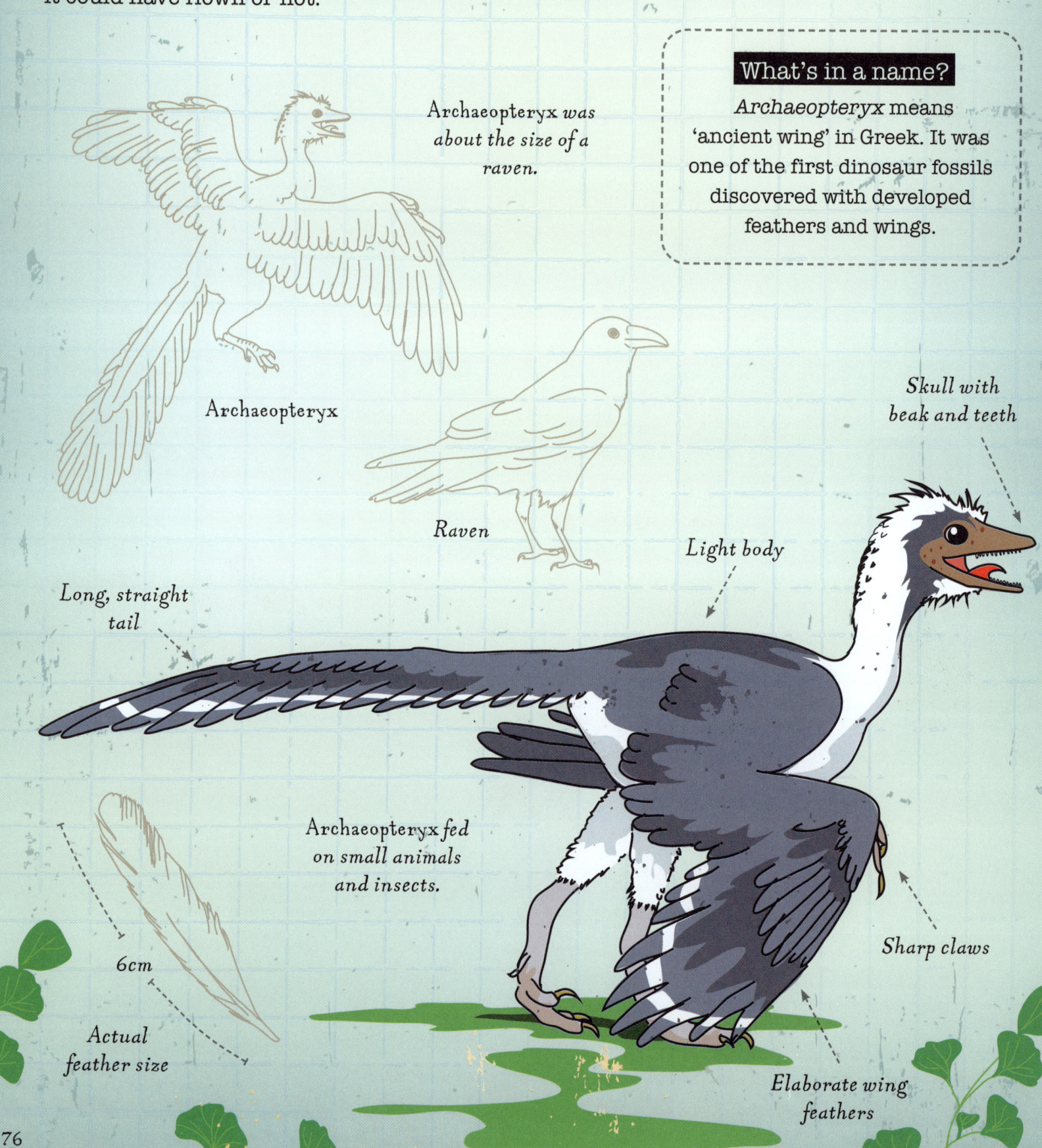

Archaeopteryx was about the size of a raven.

What's in a name?
Archaeopteryx means 'ancient wing' in Greek. It was one of the first dinosaur fossils discovered with developed feathers and wings.

Archaeopteryx

Raven

Skull with beak and teeth

Light body

Long, straight tail

Archaeopteryx fed on small animals and insects.

6cm

Actual feather size

Sharp claws

Elaborate wing feathers

Iguanodon bernissartensis

Family: Ornithopod • Period: Cretaceous
Pronunciation: Ig-wan-o-don bern-is-sart-en-sis

One of the first dinosaurs ever discovered, *Iguanodon*'s fossil remains were unearthed in 1825 before scientists even knew what dinosaurs were. It was a bulky plant-eater with a beak and large thumb spikes, used for digging food or fighting predators. Its remains helped scientists to identify dinosaurs as a group.

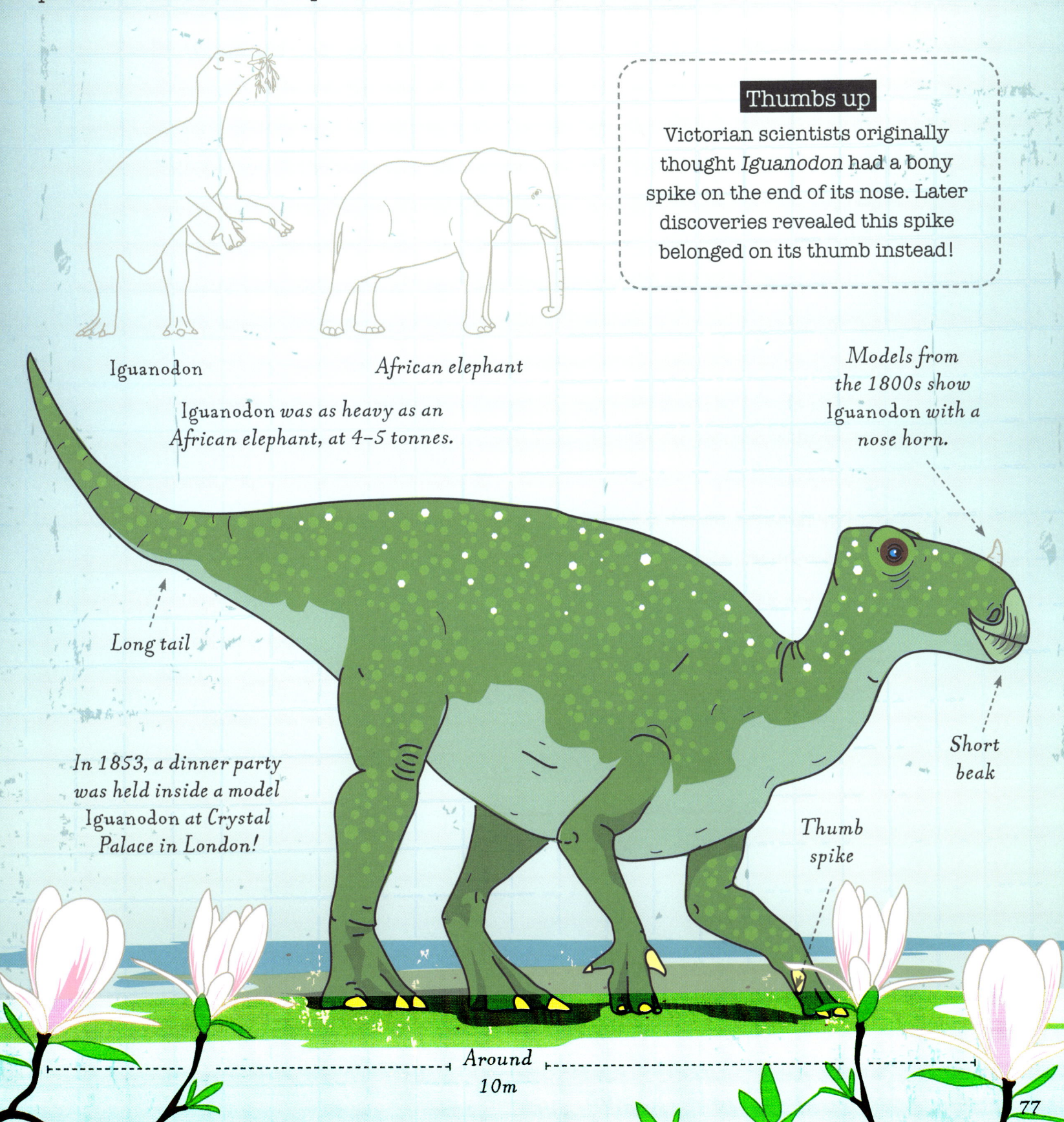

Iguanodon

African elephant

Iguanodon was as heavy as an African elephant, at 4–5 tonnes.

Thumbs up

Victorian scientists originally thought *Iguanodon* had a bony spike on the end of its nose. Later discoveries revealed this spike belonged on its thumb instead!

Models from the 1800s show Iguanodon with a nose horn.

Long tail

In 1853, a dinner party was held inside a model Iguanodon at Crystal Palace in London!

Short beak

Thumb spike

Around 10m

Scelidosaurus harrisonii

Family: Ornithopod • Period: Jurassic
Pronunciation: Ske-ly-doh-saw-rus har-ris-son-e-eye

Scelidosaurus is one of the best known species of early ornithischians. We know it best from a beautifully preserved and near-complete skeleton found in the UK. This armoured plant-eater was an early ancestor of all other armoured ornithischians, including *Stegosaurus* and *Ankylosaurus*.

Family connection

Scelidosaurus was part of a group of ornithischian dinosaurs called 'thyreopherans' – or 'shield bearers' in Greek. This name refers to their thick armour plating.

The best preserved Scelidosaurus fossil ever was discovered in Dorset, UK, in 2000.

UK

Row of spikes down back

Scelidosaurus was covered in bony scutes hard enough to break a predator's teeth.

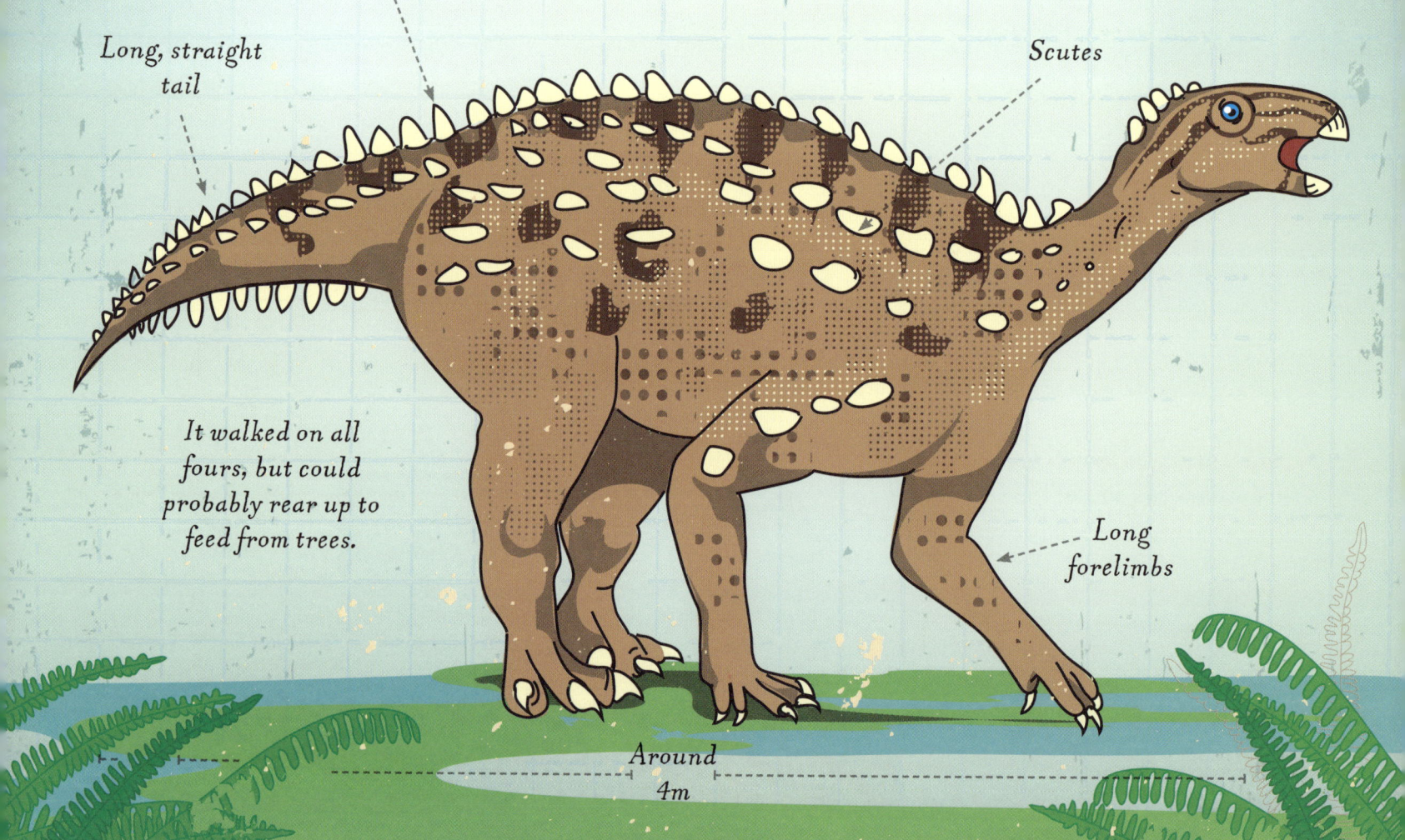

Long, straight tail

Scutes

It walked on all fours, but could probably rear up to feed from trees.

Long forelimbs

Around 4m

Hatzegopteryx thambema

Family: Pterosaur • Period: Cretaceous
Pronunciation: Hat-seg-op-ter-iks tham-bee-ma

Hatzegopteryx grew to an enormous size with a wingspan of 10–12 metres. Living towards the end of the Cretaceous, it was probably the top predator on the islands that used to cover Europe. It was so big that it even preyed on dinosaurs, snapping them up and carrying them away in its huge beak.

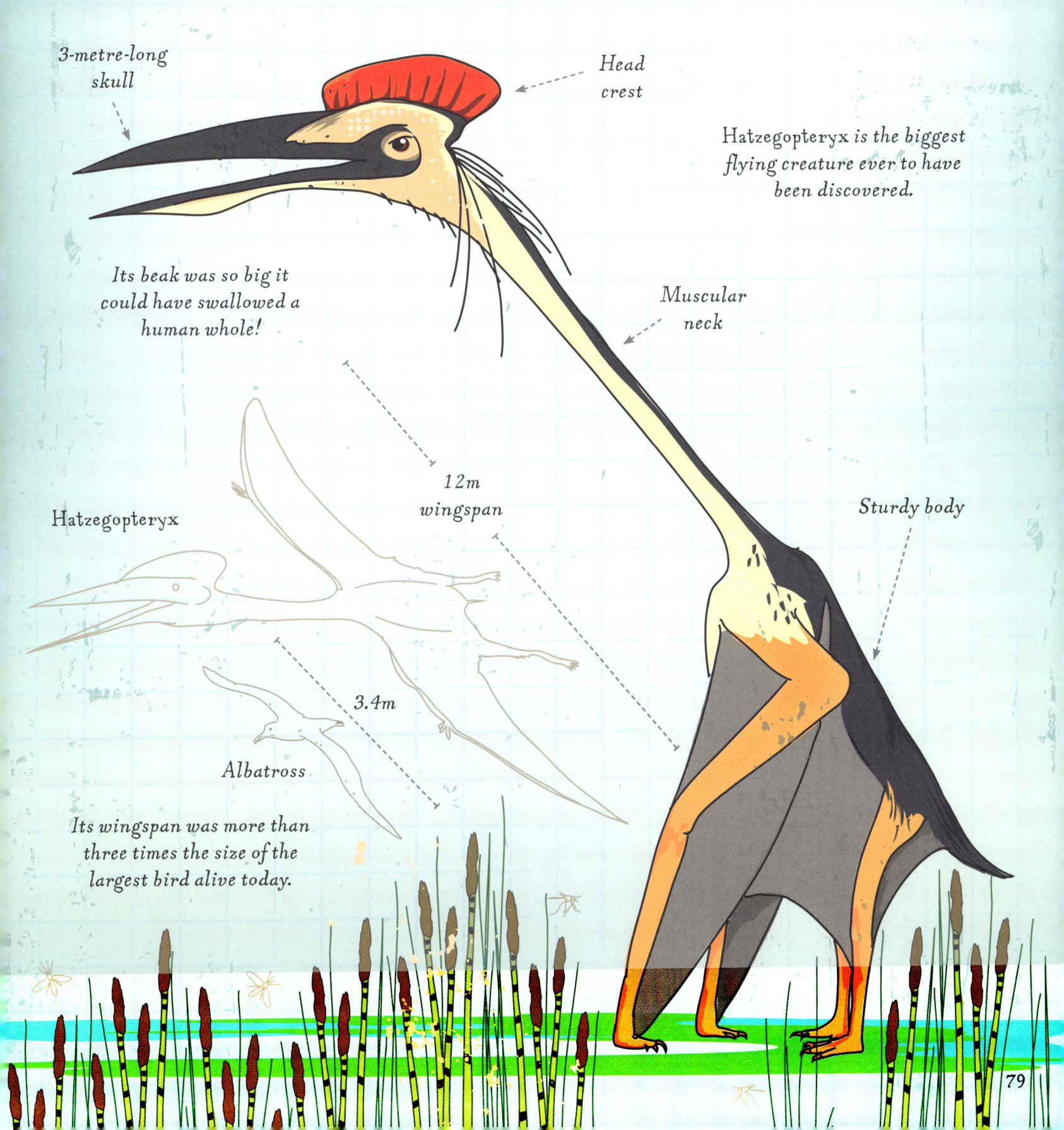

3-metre-long skull

Head crest

Hatzegopteryx is the biggest flying creature ever to have been discovered.

Its beak was so big it could have swallowed a human whole!

Muscular neck

12m wingspan

Hatzegopteryx

Sturdy body

3.4m

Albatross

Its wingspan was more than three times the size of the largest bird alive today.

Ornithocheirus simus

Family: Pterosaur • Period: Cretaceous
Pronunciation: Awn-ith-o-ky-rus sy-mus

Ornithocheirus lived along the coast on the group of islands that stood where Europe's mainland is today. This pterosaur had a distinctively crested jaw, which might have been used to cut through water as it hunted for fish. It could then impale prey on its spear-like teeth.

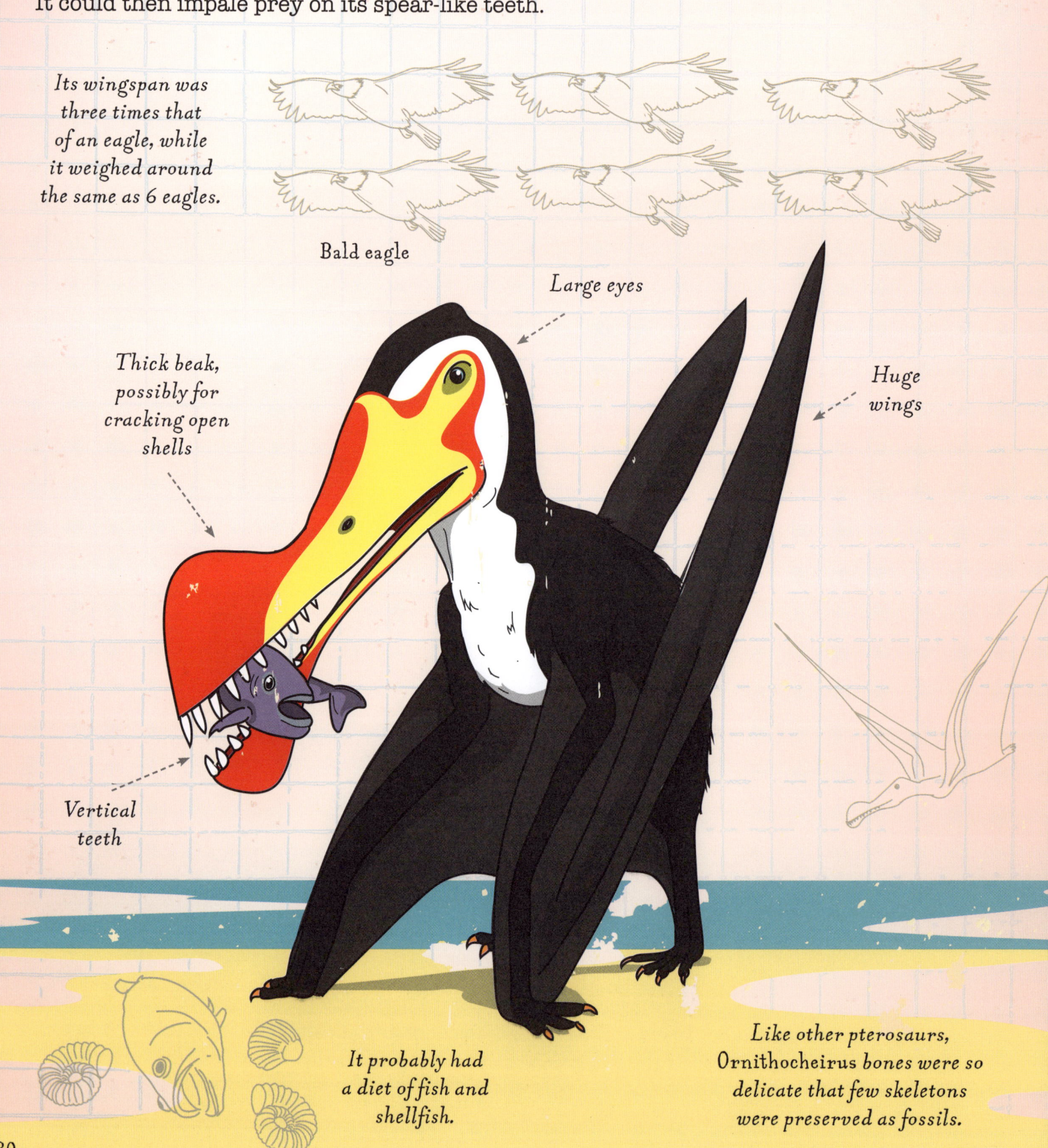

Its wingspan was three times that of an eagle, while it weighed around the same as 6 eagles.

Bald eagle

Large eyes

Thick beak, possibly for cracking open shells

Huge wings

Vertical teeth

It probably had a diet of fish and shellfish.

Like other pterosaurs, *Ornithocheirus* bones were so delicate that few skeletons were preserved as fossils.

Liopleurodon ferox

Family: Pliosaur • Period: Jurassic
Pronunciation: Li-o-plur-o-don feh-roks

Patrolling the seas of Jurassic Europe, *Liopleurodon* was the top predator of the oceans at the time and the largest species of its kind ever to live. It had a large skull with powerful jaws, and moved its bulky body through the water with strong, paddle-like limbs. Most of its fossils have been found in England and France.

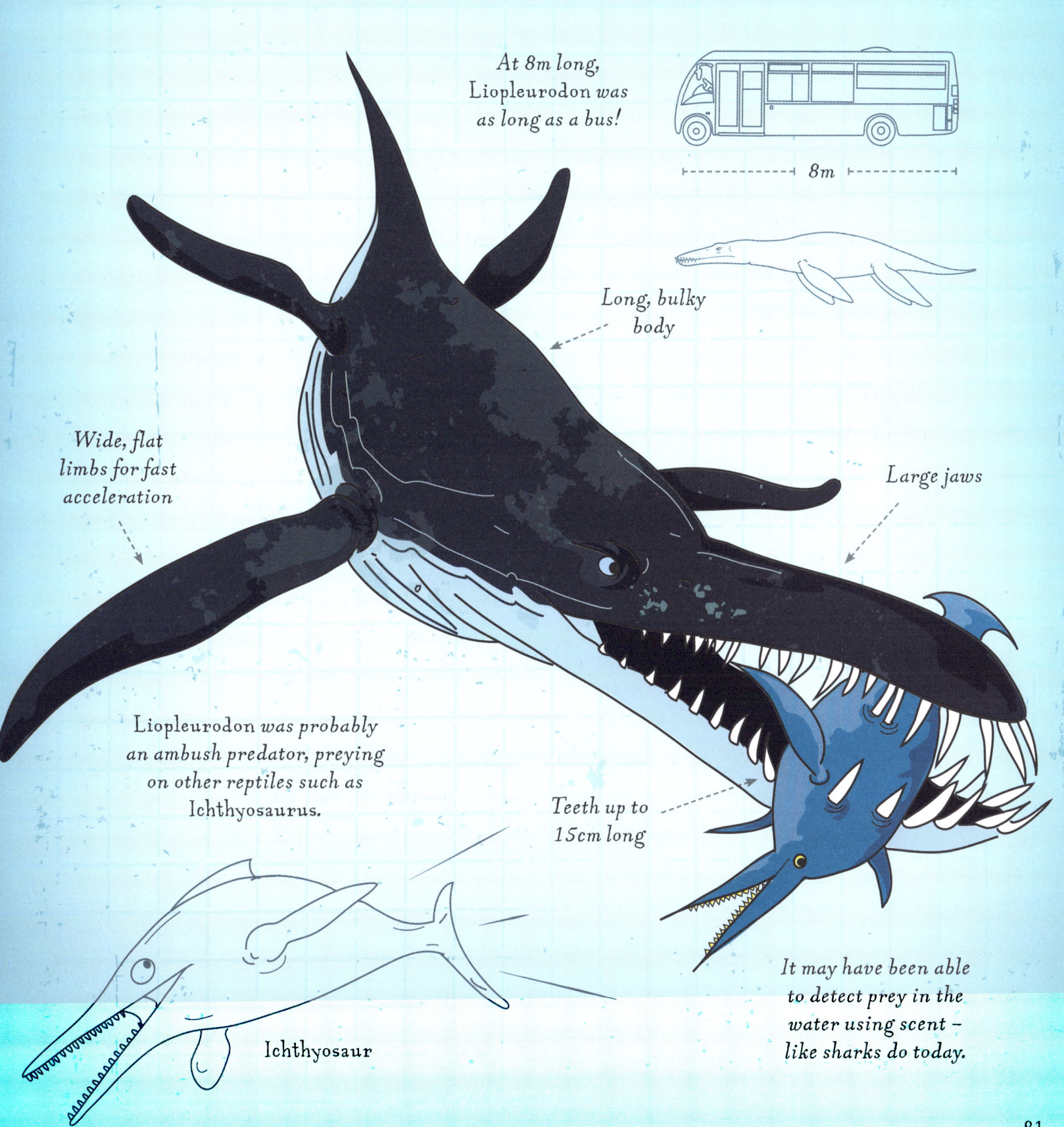

At 8m long, Liopleurodon was as long as a bus!

8m

Long, bulky body

Wide, flat limbs for fast acceleration

Large jaws

Liopleurodon was probably an ambush predator, preying on other reptiles such as Ichthyosaurus.

Teeth up to 15cm long

Ichthyosaur

It may have been able to detect prey in the water using scent – like sharks do today.

81

Plesiosaurus dolichodeirus

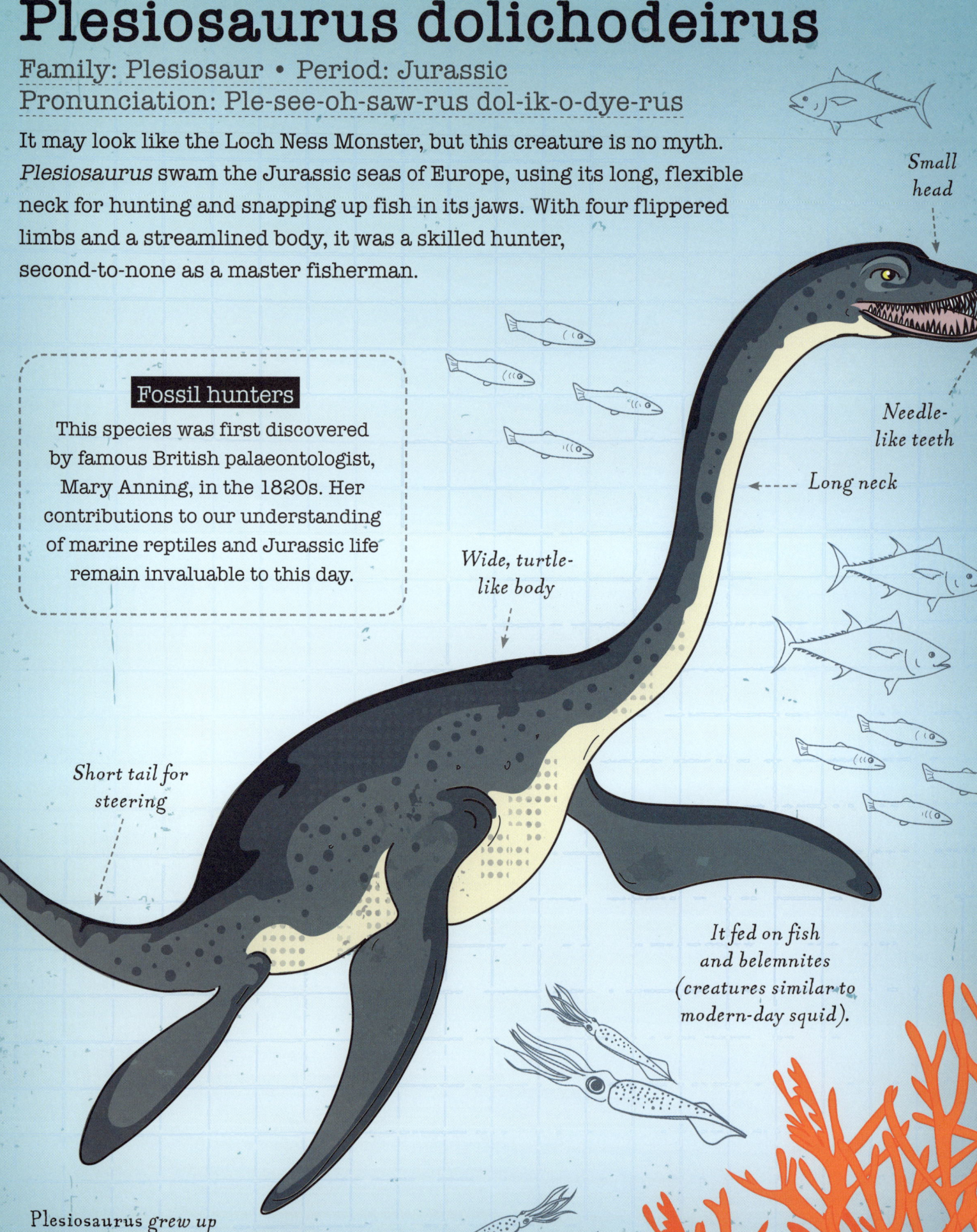

Family: Plesiosaur • Period: Jurassic
Pronunciation: Ple-see-oh-saw-rus dol-ik-o-dye-rus

It may look like the Loch Ness Monster, but this creature is no myth. *Plesiosaurus* swam the Jurassic seas of Europe, using its long, flexible neck for hunting and snapping up fish in its jaws. With four flippered limbs and a streamlined body, it was a skilled hunter, second-to-none as a master fisherman.

Fossil hunters

This species was first discovered by famous British palaeontologist, Mary Anning, in the 1820s. Her contributions to our understanding of marine reptiles and Jurassic life remain invaluable to this day.

Small head

Needle-like teeth

Long neck

Wide, turtle-like body

Short tail for steering

It fed on fish and belemnites (creatures similar to modern-day squid).

Plesiosaurus grew up to 5 metres long – the length of a great white shark today.

Metriorhynchus superciliosus

Family: Crocodyliform • Period: Jurassic
Pronunciation: Met-ree-oh-rink-us soo-per-sil-ee-oh-sus

Unlike modern crocodiles, *Metriorhynchus* spent all of its life out at sea. It was incredibly well adapted for this life, as it was able to filter saltwater and had flippered limbs for agility in the open. It also had a mouth full of sharp teeth for hunting marine prey.

Salt glands between the snout and eyes enabled it to drink salty seawater.

Fin-like tail

Long snout for catching fish

Strong flippers for swimming

Metriorhynchus was similar in size to modern crocodiles but had a streamlined body and a finned tail like a dolphin.

3m

Metriorhynchus

Crocodile

Dolphin

Ammonite

Its diet consisted of ammonites and fish.

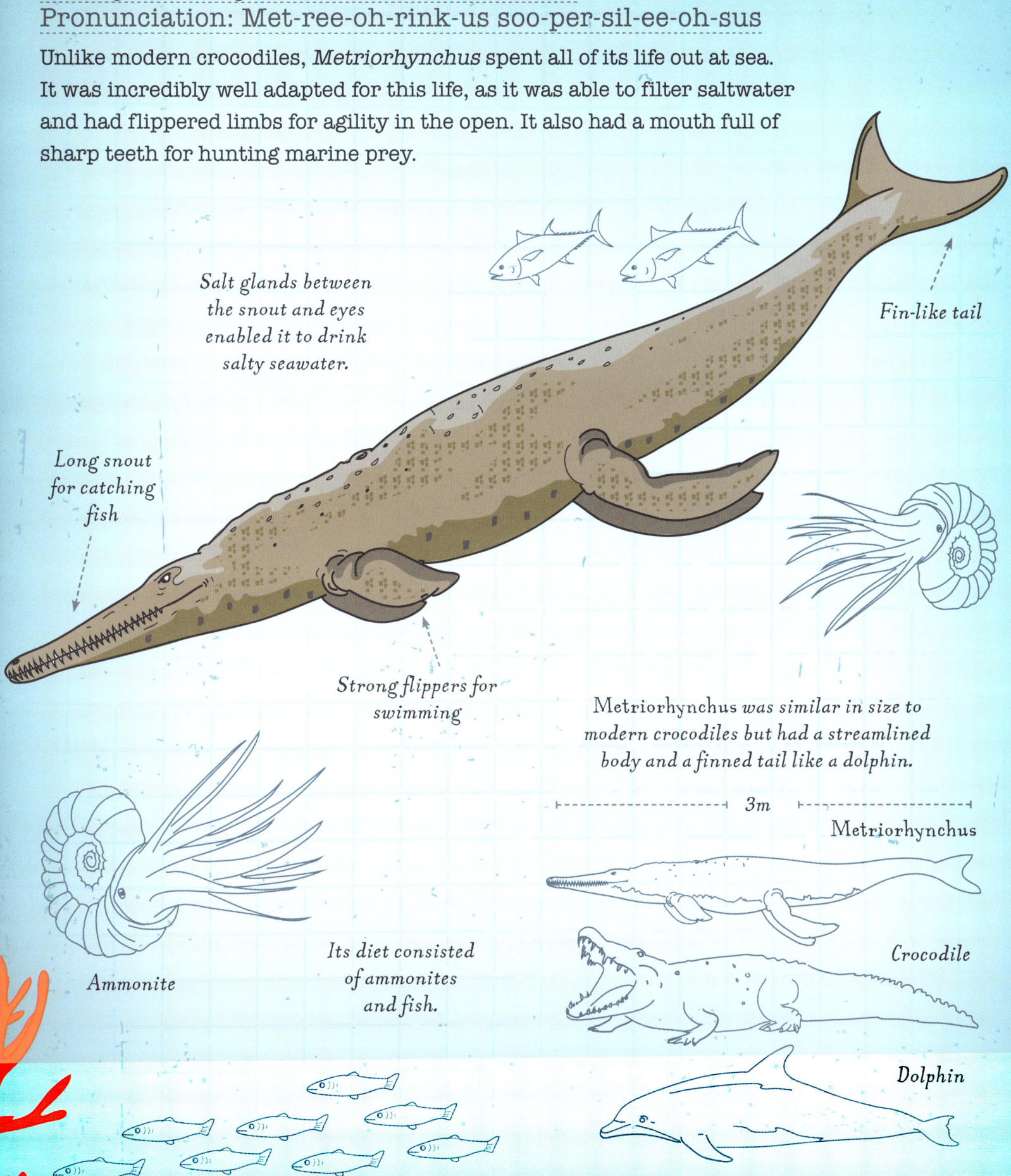

83

INDIAN OCEAN

Key

1. Australovenator wintonensis
2. Leaellynasaura amicagraphica
3. Minmi paravertebra
4. Vegasaurus molyi
5. Kronosaurus queenslandicus
6. Savannasaurus Elliottorum

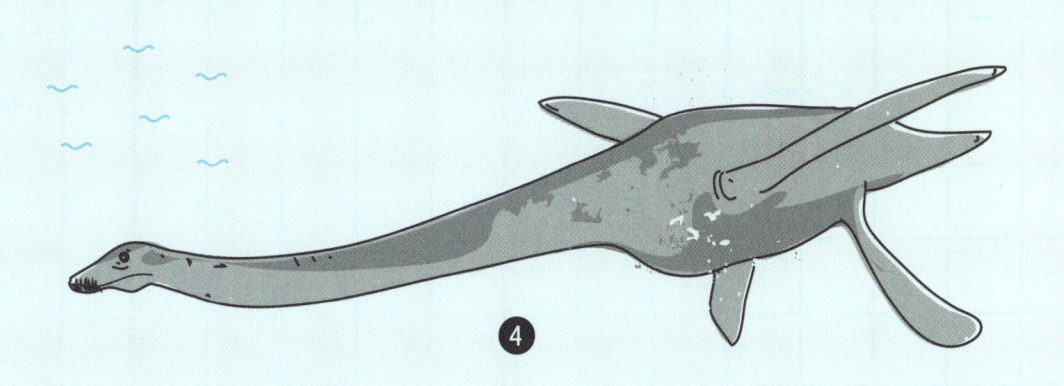

Oceania

Australia and Antarctica remained joined together throughout the Triassic, Jurassic and Cretaceous periods. Close to the South Pole, the region experienced cool and even freezing temperatures and long, dark nights. However, it still would have been covered in thick forests and dinosaurs lived right across the continent. Dinosaurs from the western side of the continent would have been able to migrate north across land bridges to South America. They may have flocked north in winter to escape the cold conditions.

TASMAN SEA

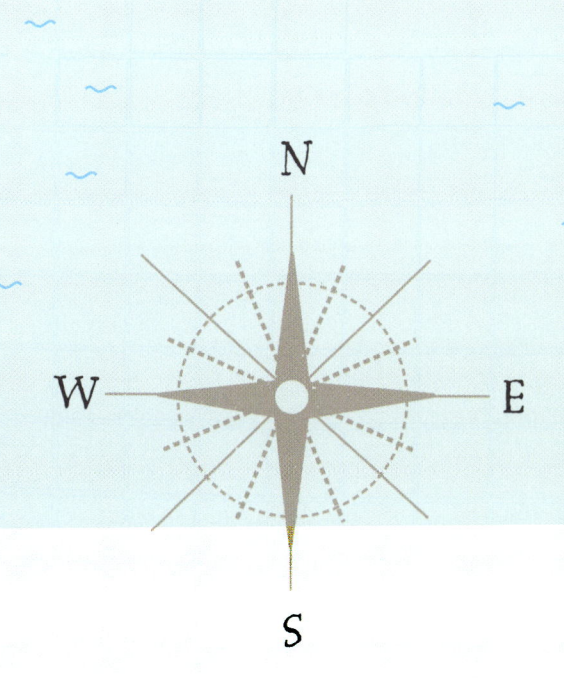

N
W   E
S

Australovenator wintonensis

Group: Theropod • Period: Cretaceous
Pronunciation: Os-trah-loh-ven-ah-tore win-ton-en-sis

Australovenator was a large, lightly built predator that sprinted after prey, much like large cats do today. In fact its speed has earned it the nickname 'cheetah of its time'! It lived in a period when Australia and Antarctica were still connected together as a single continent, so it probably roamed freely across both continents.

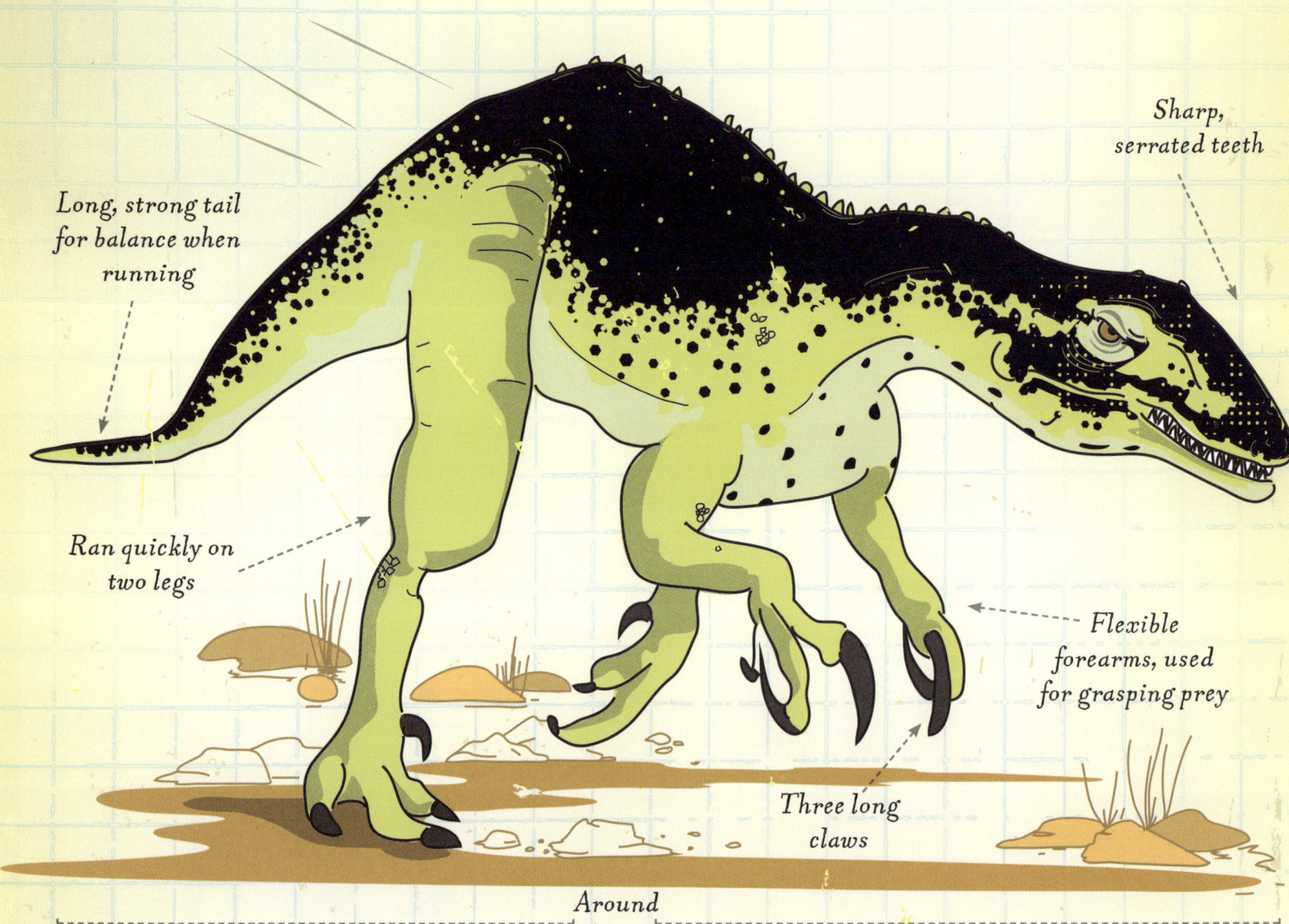

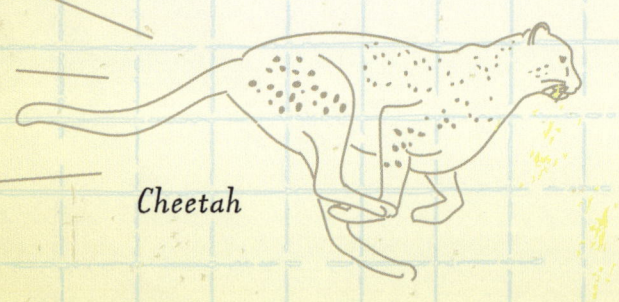

Sharp, serrated teeth

Long, strong tail for balance when running

Ran quickly on two legs

Flexible forearms, used for grasping prey

Three long claws

Around 6m

Cheetah

Like cheetahs today, Australovenator was a fast runner, relying on speed to catch prey.

Stampede!
At Lark Quarry in Australia, hundreds of footprints have been found that are thought to represent a dinosaur stampede! *Australovenator* was found nearby, so palaeontologists guess the stampede started as dinosaurs ran away from it.

Savannasaurus elliottorum

Group: Sauropod • Period: Cretaceous
Pronunciation: Sah-vah-nah-sore-us ell-ee-oh-tore-um

Reaching lengths of around 15 metres, *Savannasaurus* was one of the largest dinosaurs known from Cretaceous Australia. The huge plant-eater lived alongside predators such as *Australovenator*, so its size would have been a great advantage for defence.

It is thought that dinosaurs like Savannasaurus may have migrated between South America and Australia, thanks to a land bridge across Antarctica.

What's in a name?
The environment in which *Savannasaurus* lived closely resembled the hot, dry conditions of the savannah in modern-day Africa.

Savannasaurus had very wide hips. Each hip bone was more than 1 metre wide!

Small head

Long neck lightened by air pockets

Long, whip-like tail for defence

Only one Savannasaurus fossil has ever been found. It took 10 years to excavate it from the rock encasing it.

Massive, barrel-like ribcage housing huge organs

Leaellynasaura amicagraphica

Group: Ornithopod • Period: Cretaceous
Pronunciation: Lee-ell-in-ah-sore-ah ah-mih-cah-graph-ick-ah

This Antarctic dinosaur was well-adapted to living in the cold and dark, with feather-like bristles for insulation and large eyes for good night vision. At the time *Leaellynasaura* lived, the Antarctic circle had lighter summers and darker winters than it does now. This is because the angle of the Earth's tilt was more extreme than it is today.

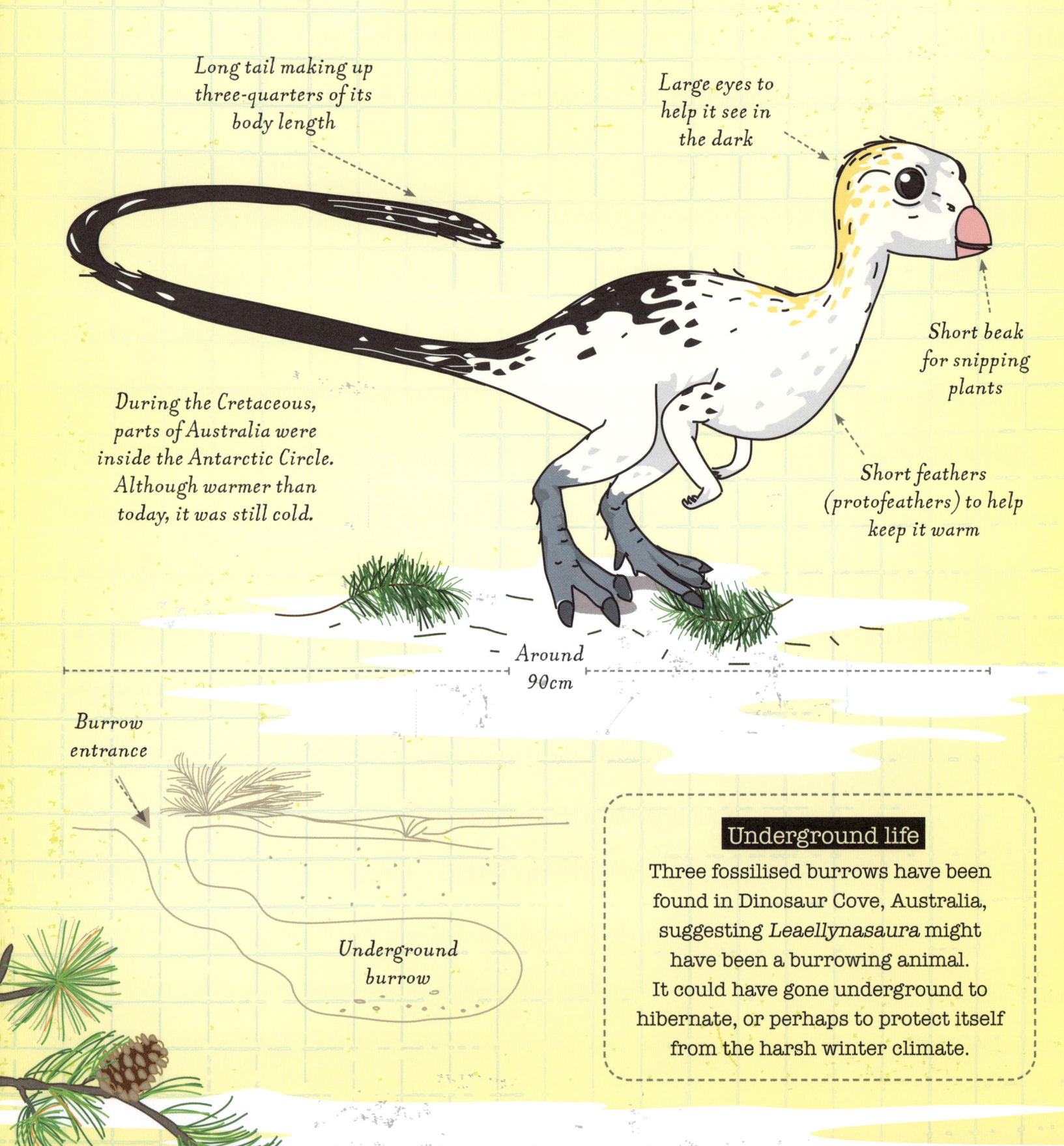

Long tail making up three-quarters of its body length

Large eyes to help it see in the dark

Short beak for snipping plants

During the Cretaceous, parts of Australia were inside the Antarctic Circle. Although warmer than today, it was still cold.

Short feathers (protofeathers) to help keep it warm

Around 90cm

Burrow entrance

Underground burrow

Underground life

Three fossilised burrows have been found in Dinosaur Cove, Australia, suggesting *Leaellynasaura* might have been a burrowing animal. It could have gone underground to hibernate, or perhaps to protect itself from the harsh winter climate.

Minmi paravertebra

Group: Ornithopod • Period: Cretaceous
Pronunciation: Min-mee pah-rah-ver-tuh-brah

Minmi was an armoured dinosaur, but was much smaller than its cousins in North America. The plant-eater weighed around 300kg – only one-twentieth the size of an African elephant. For an ankylosaur, it had relatively long limbs, to help it run away when a quick escape was needed. Unlike most other ankylosaurs, it also had belly armour.

Named and described in 1980, Minmi was the first ankylosaur discovered in the Southern Hemisphere.

2.7m — 3m

Minmi was only just longer than a Smart Car.

Bony scutes running down back

Spikes

Unlike fellow ankylosaurs, it had no armour on its skull.

Thin bony rods along the inside of its tail might have attached to muscles to strengthen the spine.

No tail club (unlike other ankylosaurs)

Beaked mouth

Long limbs suggest it could have run quickly.

Kronosaurus queenslandicus

Group: Pliosaur • Period: Cretaceous
Pronunciation: Croh-noh-sore-us kweens-land-ick-us

A true titan of the seas, *Kronosaurus* was a terrifying apex predator. It had a short neck, powerful jaws and a large body propelled through the seas by strong flippers. Between its limbs were a series of belly ribs, offering additional support as it swam through the oceans.

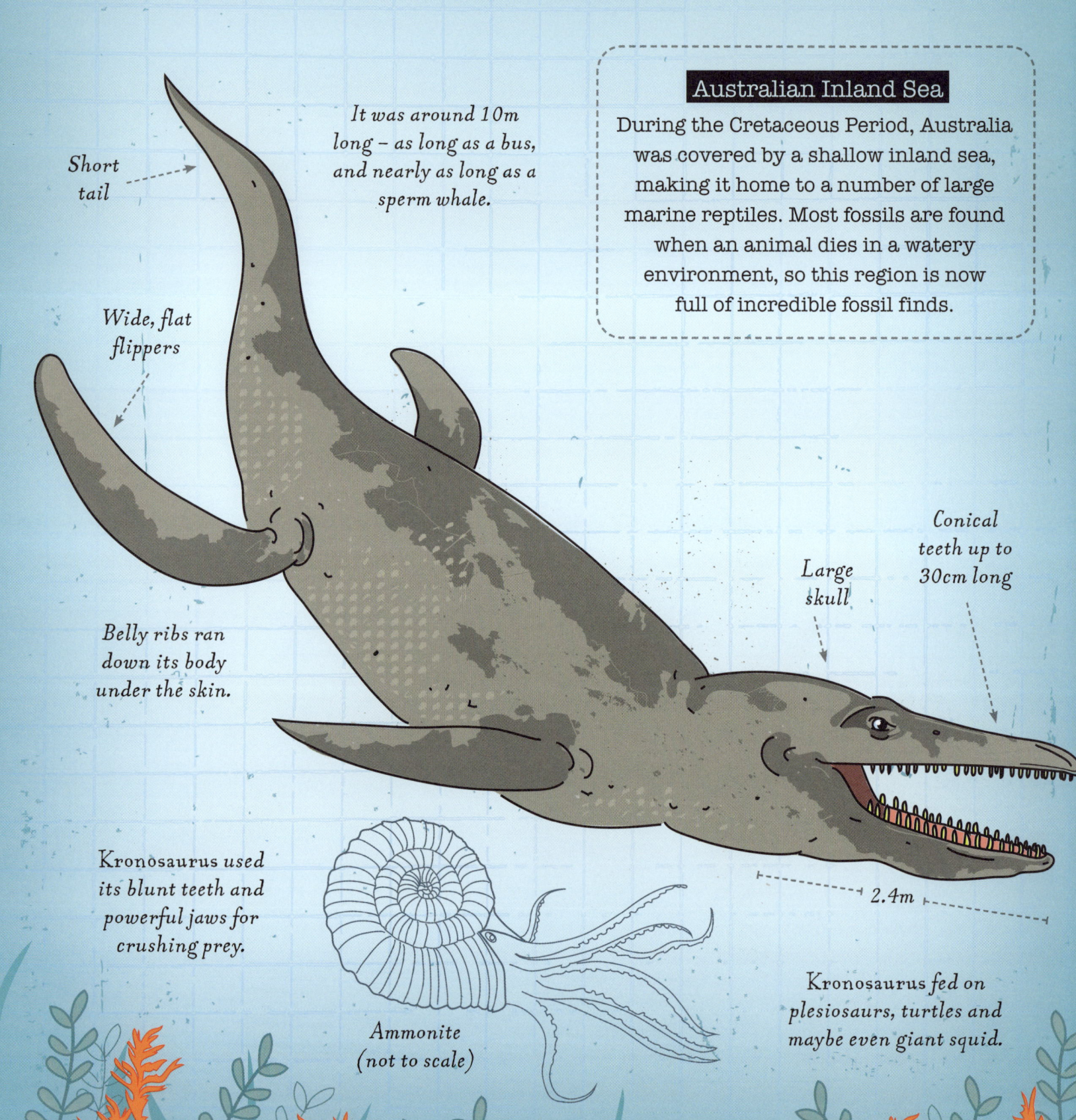

Short tail

It was around 10m long – as long as a bus, and nearly as long as a sperm whale.

Australian Inland Sea

During the Cretaceous Period, Australia was covered by a shallow inland sea, making it home to a number of large marine reptiles. Most fossils are found when an animal dies in a watery environment, so this region is now full of incredible fossil finds.

Wide, flat flippers

Belly ribs ran down its body under the skin.

Large skull

Conical teeth up to 30cm long

Kronosaurus used its blunt teeth and powerful jaws for crushing prey.

Ammonite (not to scale)

2.4m

Kronosaurus fed on plesiosaurs, turtles and maybe even giant squid.

Vegasaurus molyi

Group: Plesiosaur • Period: Cretaceous
Pronunciation: Vey-ga-sore-us moh-lee-eye

Back in a time when marine reptiles ruled the Antarctic seas, *Vegasaurus* was one of the top hunters around. It had a long, mobile neck and a streamlined body for stealthily gliding through water as it hunted fish and other smaller marine reptiles.

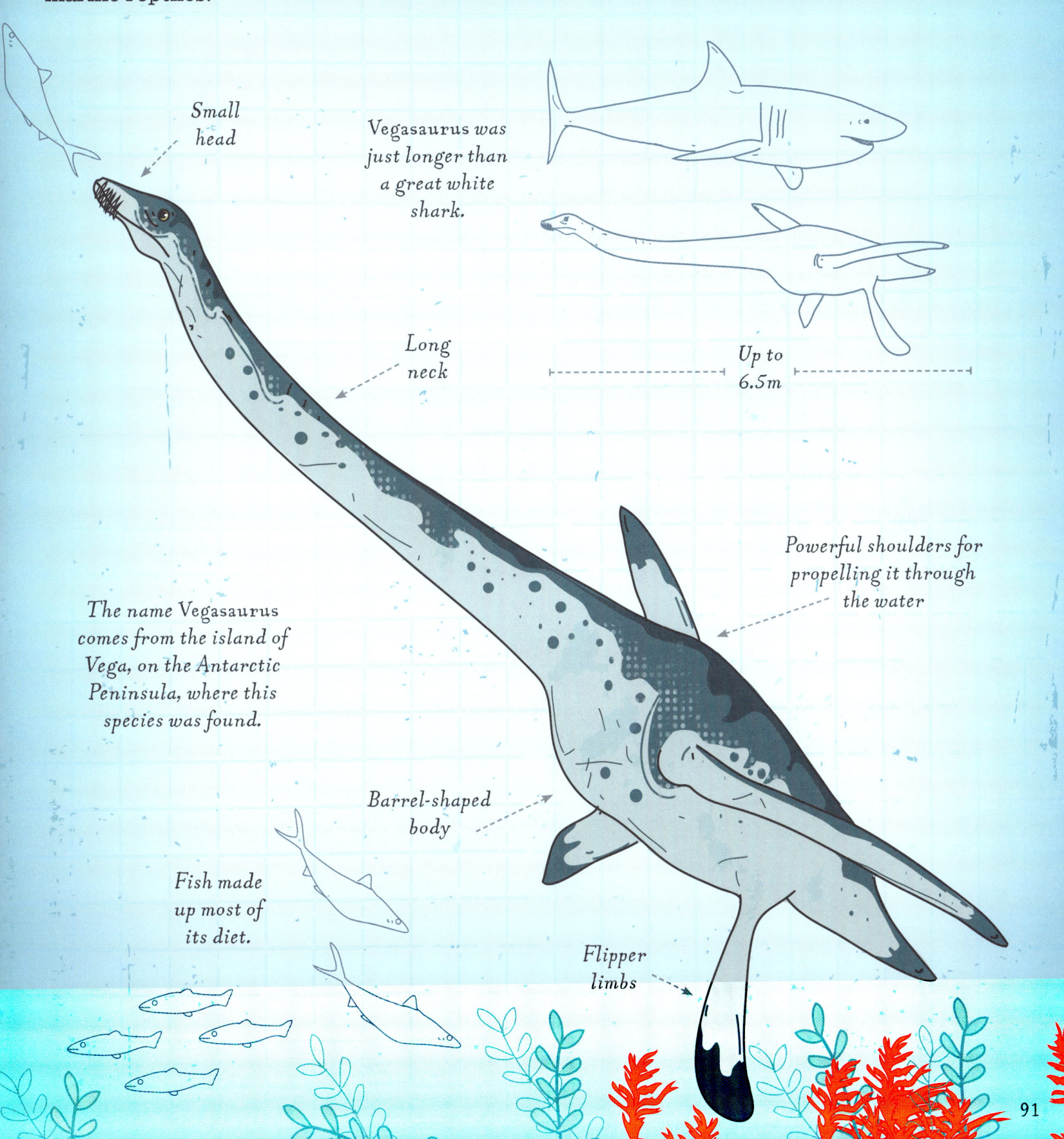

Small head

Vegasaurus was just longer than a great white shark.

Long neck

Up to 6.5m

Powerful shoulders for propelling it through the water

The name Vegasaurus comes from the island of Vega, on the Antarctic Peninsula, where this species was found.

Barrel-shaped body

Fish made up most of its diet.

Flipper limbs

91

Glossary

Archosaur
The reptile group that includes dinosaurs, pterosaurs and crocodiles.

Bipedal
An animal that uses two legs for walking. Some dinosaurs were bipedal; others walked on four legs some of the time but could also run on two legs.

Carnivore
An animal that naturally feeds only on meat.

Extinction
When a species or group of animals has no living members. There was a mass extinction event at the end of the Cretaceous Period.

Fossil
The remains or impressions of a plant or animal preserved in rock.

Herbivore
An animal that naturally feeds only on plants.

Mammal
A warm-blooded animal that has hair or fur and feeds its young with milk. The first mammals appeared towards the end of the age of the dinosaurs.

Marine reptile
A prehistoric swimming reptile from the age of the dinosaurs. Marine reptiles were not dinosaurs at all, but were a separate group of animals. They had to come to the surface to breathe air.

Mesozoic Era
The geological period from 251 million years ago to 66 million years ago, during which the dinosaurs lived. The Mesozoic Era is split into three further periods: the Triassic, the Jurassic and the Cretaceous.

Meteor
A small icy and rocky object that enters the Earth's atmosphere.

Omnivore
An animal that eats both plants and other animals.

Ornithischian
'Bird-hipped' dinosaurs with backward-slanting hip bones. Ornithischians were all plant-eaters. Some had armour or horns.

Ornithopod
A mainly bipedal and herbivorous dinosaur.

Palaeontologist
A scientist that studies the fossil record.

Predator
An animal that naturally preys on other animals.

Pterosaur
A prehistoric flying reptile from the age of the dinosaurs. Pterosaurs were not dinosaurs at all, but a separate group of animals.

Quadrupedal
An animal that walks on all four of its legs.

Reptile
A scaly group of animals including snakes, lizards, crocodiles, tortoises, turtles and dinosaurs. Reptiles typically have scaly skin and lay eggs.

Saurischian
'Lizard-hipped' dinosaurs with forward-slanting hip bones. Saurischians were made up of two further groups: sauropods and theropods.

Sauropod
These were usually large, quadrupedal dinosaurs with long necks and tails.

Scutes
A bony protective plate on the back of some dinosaurs.

Thagomizer
The name given to the spikes on the tails of stegosaurs.

Theropod
Typically carnivorous and bipedal dinosaurs.

Index

Age of Dinosaurs 8–9
Alcione elainus 51
Allosaurus fragilis 15
Amargasaurus cazaui 35
ammonites 11, 83, 90
Angolasaurus bocagei 52
Anhanguera blittersdorffi 38
ankylosaurs 78, 89
Anning, Mary 82
Antarctic dinosaurs 88
Archaeopteryx lithographica 76
Archelon ischyros 26
archosaurs 8, 30
armour 7
  see also horns; osteoderms; plates, bony; scutes; spikes and spines
Australovenator wintonensis 86
Azhdarcho lancicollis 68

Balaur bondoc 75
Baryonyx walkeri 72
belemnites 82
birds 7, 8, 9, 76
bite force 14, 53
Brachiosaurus altithorax 18
brains 14, 21, 31
bristles 56, 88
burrows 88

Caihong juji 59
camouflage 56, 65
cannibalism 44

Carcharodontosaurus 48
  C. saharicus 43
Carnotaurus sastrei 32
cephalopods 69
ceratopsians 64, 65
claws 14, 16, 25, 31, 43, 45, 57, 58, 72, 75
colours 56, 59
Compsognathus longipes 74
coprolites 11
Cretaceous period 8, 9
crocodiles 6, 8, 14, 39, 42, 53, 83
cycads 23
cynodonts 30

Dakosaurus andiniensis 39
Dakotaraptor steini 16
Diplodocus carnegii 19
displays 20, 59, 67
Dreadnoughtus schrani 36

eggs 6, 7, 11, 18, 45, 57
Eoraptor lunensis 33
extinction 9

faeces (poo) 11
feathers 7, 9, 11, 16, 17, 57, 58, 59, 76, 88
flying reptiles *see* pterosaurs
fossils 7, 10–11, 62, 90
  formation 10
  trace fossils 11
fur 74

Giganotosaurus carolinii 31
Giraffatitan 18
Gondwana 8, 54
Guidraco venator 67

Halszkaraptor escuilliei 60
Hatzegopteryx thambema 79

head crests 15, 17, 20, 25, 31, 50, 59, 67, 73, 79
head and neck frills 23, 64
herds 23, 64
Herrerasaurus ischigualastensis 30
heterodonty 33
hip bones 7, 87
horns 7, 23, 32, 44
Huabeisaurus allocotus 61
Huayangosaurus taibaii 63

ichthyosaurs 39, 52, 69, 81
Iguanodon 48
  I. bernissartensis 77
intelligence 17

jaws 15, 42, 44, 80
Jurassic period 8, 9

Kentrosaurus aethiopicus 49
keratin 65, 78
Kronosaurus queenslandicus 90
Kryptodrakon progenitor 66

Laurasia 8, 54
Leaellynasaura amicagraphica 88
Lesothosaurus diagnosticus 47
Liliensternus liliensterni 73
Liopleurodon ferox 81
lizards 6, 27, 33, 52, 74

Majungasaurus crenatissimus 44
Mamenchisaurus constructus 62
marine reptiles 39
  see also ichthyosaurs; mosasaurs; plesiosaurs; pliosaurs